GW00891085

CONTENTS

Note: County/Area

Although in some parts of the British Isles, Scout Counties are known as Areas or Islands, in one case Bailiwick, and from 1 April 2008 in Scotland, a Region, for ease of reading this resource we simply refer to County or Counties.

INTRODUCTION

WELCOME TO *THE TROOP PROGRAMME.*
WE HOPE IT WILL PROVIDE YOU WITH MANY OF
THE TOOLS, IDEAS AND TECHNIQUES NEEDED TO
RUN AN EXCITING BALANCED PROGRAMME FOR
YOUR SCOUT TROOP.

You can use the material to challenge and inspire your Scouts, to get them interested in areas they may not have previously considered. *The Troop Programme* also includes requirements for all the awards and badges available to Scouts.

It has been written for all adult Leaders and Assistants working within the Scout Troop. It would equally be of value to Young Leaders working in the Section, as well as your Patrol Leaders.

The Troop Programme is one of four resources for adults working with Scout Troops:

- *Troop Essentials* is the indispensable guide to the day to day running of a Scout Troop. There are chapters covering leadership teams, young people, everyday adventure, communication and image, administration and a comprehensive appendix.

- *The Troop Programme Plus* is the paper counterpart to Programmes Online (www.scouts.org.uk/pol) the popular online resource for programme material. *The Troop Programme Plus* (volumes one and two) provides a fresh and evergreen selection of practical programme ideas, games and skill instructions for use with your Scout Troop - don't try planning programmes without it!

HOW TO USE THIS BOOK

Although you may wish to read *The Troop Programme* from cover to cover, it may be helpful to just dip in and out as required. But don't keep it to yourself; make sure all your team has access to copies. All four publications have been written with the new Leader in mind so also make them available to potential Assistants.

The Troop Programme is intended to provide information and guidance that will help you to deliver a Balanced Programme that everyone in your Troop will enjoy. The content of this resource has been written as an aid; use it with confidence and don't be afraid to try unfamiliar activities.

There may be some words or phrases in these resources with which you are unfamiliar. We have therefore included a glossary at the end. A more comprehensive glossary can be found in *Troop Essentials*. If there is anything else that you are unsure of, other adults in Scouting will always be happy to help, so don't be afraid to ask, or contact the Scout Information Centre on 0845 300 1818 or at info.centre@scout.org.uk.

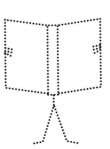

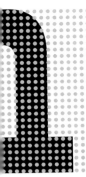

PROGRAMME PLANNING

YOUNG PEOPLE JOIN A SCOUT TROOP FOR MANY REASONS. IT MIGHT SIMPLY BE THE NEXT STEP AFTER CUB SCOUTS OR THEY MIGHT HAVE HEARD GOOD THINGS FROM THEIR FRIENDS. PERHAPS PARENTS OR CARERS ARE VERY KEEN FOR THEIR CHILDREN TO JOIN AS THEY REMEMBER THE GREAT TIME THEY HAD IN SCOUTING.

Whatever the reason your Scouts have for joining the Troop, whether or not they stay will be down to you and your team, and the programme you provide week after week. Many young people today have busy lives and high expectations, but when a Troop offers an exciting Balanced Programme, young people will be eager to take part. Young people want to be part of something active, lively and fun. They want to learn new skills, enjoy games and challenges and experience some excitement and adventure. They want to be with a group of friends, and they are anxious to build their confidence and prove their ability. As they grow older, they will want to experience a little responsibility and from time to time take charge. Their views matter, and they will want to have the opportunity to influence what they do.

All adults in Scouting need to remember that the most precious possession a young person has is their time. Unless we provide an enjoyable Balanced Programme, the young person will probably leave to do something else instead.

OVERVIEW OF THE BALANCED PROGRAMME

The Scout Association has a Programme that aims to promote the growth and development of young people. Providing young people with a programme that is balanced and rewarding is one of our greatest challenges as Leaders. The Balanced Programme is defined from the perspective of a young person:

Young people experience Scouting by regularly taking part in quality activities, drawn from each Programme Zone. Personal achievement can be recognised through earning awards and badges leading to Chief Scout's Awards and the Queen's Scout Award.

What do we mean by 'Programme'?

In Scouting, the word programme has a wide interpretation. Programme is not just about the activities that Scouts can take part in (almost anything from abseiling to zorbing). It is also how we do these activities (the Methods) and why we do them (values deriving from the Scout Promise). Every time we plan an activity for our Scouts we should also consider how we might organise the activity and why we are doing it.

What we offer to young people in the Scout Section is a Balanced Programme; a range of activities, events and experiences built around six Programme Zones.

The Programme is balanced in the same way a diet is balanced, not by precise measurements and timings but by simply ensuring that over a given period (a month or a term for example) that there is something from each zone in the Programme.

You may recall from *Troop Essentials* that some Leaders will plan their programme using the zones to ensure they include activities from each during the coming term. Other Leaders will use the zones as a check for balance at the end of a given period. They will then make a note to include more from whichever Programme Zone has been under-represented. Either approach is acceptable and it comes down to an individual Leader's style and preference.

THE PROGRAMME ZONES IN DETAIL

These are specific areas of activity and experience. There are six in each Section, from Beaver Scouts to Explorer Scouts. A Balanced Programme will draw ideas from each of them over time.

This may take the form of an event or activity, or it might be a specific Activity Badge or a Challenge. As you will see from the diagram, there are Activity Badges in every Programme Zone.

Programme Zones	Community	Fit for Life	Creative Expression	Global	Beliefs & Attitudes	Outdoor & Adventure	Top Award
Challenge Badges	Community	Fitness	Creative	Global	Promise	Outdoor	Chief Scout's Gold Award
						Outdoor Plus	
						Adventure	
						Expedition	
Example Activity Badges for each Programme Zone	Administrator	Athlete	Artist	Astronomer	My Faith	Angler	
	Fire Safety	Cyclist	Chef	Global Conservation	World Faith	Camper	
	Heritage	Martial Arts	Entertainer	Interpreter		Forester	
	Public Relations	Physical Recreation	Model Maker	Communicator		Hiker	
			Writer			Pioneer	
						Parascending	
						Snow Sports	

1. Beliefs and Attitudes

This zone provides opportunities to explore and develop Scouting values, personal attitudes and a range of beliefs. It is at the heart of all our Scouting activities.

The Promise Challenge can be achieved in this zone.

2. Community

This zone helps Scouts explore the community in which they live, discovering local people, places and facilities. It also gives them the opportunity to offer help and service.

The Community Challenge can be achieved in this zone.

3. Fit for Life

This zone focuses on activities to improve fitness, promote personal health and increase awareness of personal safety. It should provide young people with the opportunities to participate in a variety of games and to improve their skills in a range of physical pursuits.

The Fitness Challenge can be achieved in this zone.

4. Creative Expression

This zone provides opportunities for young people to display their creativity through art, music, drama, design, worship and leadership.

The Creative Challenge can be achieved in this zone.

5. Global

This zone helps Scouts to discover the similarities and differences in lifestyle, cultures and environments, both locally and from around the world. It helps them make a difference.

The Global Challenge can be achieved in this zone.

6. Outdoor and Adventure

In this, the largest zone, you will find all the activities connected with camping and the great outdoors. This zone is full of opportunities to learn, not just the traditional Scouting skills, but also those needed for adventurous activities such as climbing, caving, canoeing and sailing.

In this zone there are four Challenges that can be achieved. They are as follows:

- The Outdoor Challenge
- The Outdoor Plus Challenge
- The Adventure Challenge
- The Expedition Challenge

Almost half the Programme is made up of Outdoor and Adventure activities. The remainder comes from the other five Programme Zones.

THE METHODS

In the Programme, it is both *what you do* and *the way that you do it* that gets results. To provide variety and interest in the Programme, leadership teams will need to use a number of different Methods when working with ideas from the Programme Zones. Over a period, the leadership team should use a variety of the Methods to deliver activities. Let us explore these in more detail.

1. Activities outdoors

You should note that this does not say 'outdoor activities,' for all sorts of indoor activities can be done outside. Spending time outdoors is a good thing in itself.

2. Games

There are a huge variety of games of every type, both indoor and outdoor. There are team games, relay games, ball games, chasing games, skill games, wide games and scavenger hunts. Games can be invented or adapted to meet a range of training needs. They have many more uses than just allowing your Scouts to let off steam or fill some spare time in your programme.

3. Design and creativity

Any activity that involves building or constructing, music making, drama or dance will use design and creativity as a Method.

4. Visits and visitors

If any activity takes your Scouts to the local park, the swimming pool or a campsite, you are using this Method in your programme. Similarly, you will use this Method if an instructor, parent or carer comes to teach a special skill or to explain their hobby.

5. Service

To help other people is part of the Scout Promise. Any time your Scouts are involved in the community – from recycling waste or helping those with a disability – then you are using service as a Method to help deliver the Programme.

6. Technology and new skills

This Method is used when Scouts learn new skills or design and produce things on a small or large scale. It also applies when Scouts use information and communication technology.

7. Team-building activities

This Method is used when Scouts are working and co-operating together in groups to resolve problems and in groups to achieve an agreed goal.

8. Activities with others

Whenever your Scouts are involved with other people, whether they are others in the Scout Group, members from other youth organisations, or the wider community, they will be using this Method.

9. Themes

Imaginative and exciting story lines bring something extra to a wide game. A theme is any idea that links all or parts of a programme together by a thread, no matter how contrived!

10. Prayer, worship and reflection

This Method offers opportunities to reflect on Scouting values and experiences. It also allows you to link events in the life of the Troop to God through simple prayer, reflection and worship. Spiritual development is part of the Purpose of The Scout Association, and duty to God is an important part of the Scout Promise. A Balanced Programme will contribute to a Scout's spiritual development, just as it will to physical, intellectual and social development.

It is important that 'duty to God' is not confined to the place of worship. Scouting helps young people to be fully alive to the three great relationships in their life: self, others, and God. During their time in Scouting, Scouts need to be encouraged to grow in each of their relationships.

The bottom line

In addition to the Programme Zones and Methods, there is also a third element to the Balanced Programme, which is a measure of the outcomes of the programme and the environment in which it takes place. It underlines the Programme and is sometimes referred to as 'the bottom line'. Put simply, it identifies what people might expect to see if they walked into a Troop meeting. We need to be aware of it as it very much reflects the experience of being a Scout.

These are the elements that make up the bottom line:

- Activity: Scouts are busy, active and involved.

- Fun: Scouts are enjoying what they are doing.

- Teamwork: Scouts are involved in groups and developing a team spirit and a sense of co-operation.

- Leadership and responsibility: Older Scouts are developing leadership skills and taking on increased responsibility.

- Relationships: Scouts are learning to live together and developing friendships with other Scouts and adults.

- Commitment: Scouts are upholding the values of the Scout Promise in all that they do.

- Personal development: Scouts are learning how to cope with all the challenges they face, and improving their life skills.

THE BALANCED PROGRAMME CHECKER

At the end of an activity or Troop night, or at a planning meeting, consider filling in a Balanced Programme Checker. Put a tick in the box in the appropriate Methods column, so that it lines up against the Programme Zone it was used for. Of course, it may cover more than one zone. Also complete 'the bottom line' to reflect the experience from your Scout's point of view. Fill in one box if you thought the performance of your programme was poor, two boxes for good or three boxes for excellent.

You may find it useful to regularly transfer this information about Programme Zones and Methods to the larger chart (see below). You can then check that you are achieving a Balanced Programme. You can then plan to use as many relevant Methods as possible to deliver activities. This builds variety into the Programme, and encourages leadership teams to be imaginative in their approach.

Balanced Programme Checker - for an activity or Troop meeting

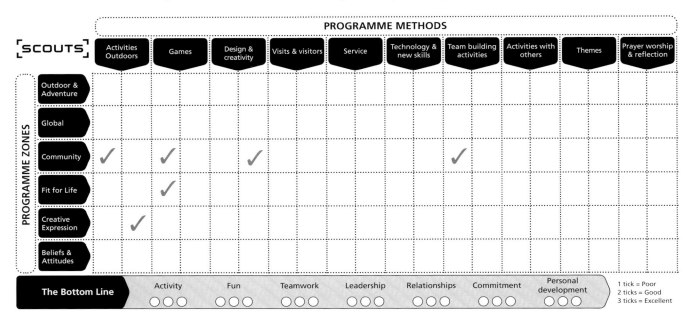

Balanced Programme Checker for a month - showing that the Global Zone is the one area in the Programme that requires some activity.

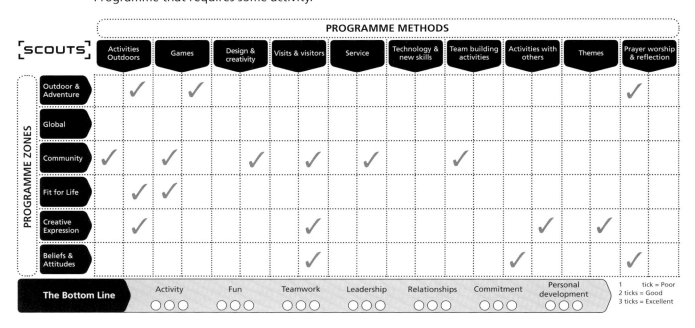

Why plan?

Most Leaders will have had the experience of putting together a Troop meeting programme at the last minute. Being spontaneous can sometimes be very effective, but it does have its drawbacks. Any programme put together at the last minute will only ever be able to use the skills and materials immediately available to hand. To really provide a wide range of opportunities and challenges that build on what has gone before, then you will need to plan and prepare over a longer period.

Annual Programme overview

The Scouting year traditionally follows the academic year, starting in September, or a little earlier in Scotland. This means that the summer camp or expedition in July or August is usually the climax of the Scouting year. Whether you follow a calendar year, or the academic year, at some stage you will need to begin the planning process for the coming year. There is no need to get into too much detail at this first attempt. You should look at some of the options for the year ahead, and identify activities and events that your Scouts might want to do.

How to produce an overview

Meet together with all the Leaders and Assistants in your team, and encourage everyone to make suggestions. This way, they will all feel they have made a contribution to the Troop's plans. Trying to plan on your own is a very lonely process, and you should try to avoid it. The following six steps will help you achieve an overview of the year ahead. The first three steps in this process do not need to be done in any particular order.

Step 1 – Note the opportunities available

- Mark on your calendar or chart all the school holidays and half-term breaks.

- Make a note also of school exam periods and any school trips.

- Mark any Leader's family time as periods that might need to be avoided.

- Mark on any national events or initiatives.

- List County or District events such as camps and competitions.

- Record any community events and opportunities that your Troop may want to be involved with.

- Add to the list any Scout Group commitments, such as the AGM or the St George's Activity Day.

Step 2 - Gather new ideas for your programme

Programme ideas may come from a wide range of sources, including books such as this one, *Scouting* and other magazines; Programmes Online, other Internet sites or, perhaps most obviously, from your Scouts! Make a list of all these programmes ideas as they come up.

Programmes Online

Programmes Online is a web-based programme-planning tool that was introduced to help Leaders plan their meetings. Leaders can share successful ideas, find new sources of inspiration and build a programme over a term or longer. Programmes Online is a way for everyone to share their ideas, and is most useful if you need a new programme activity in a hurry! Find it at www.scouts.org.uk/pol This example shows you how to use Programmes Online to gather new ideas for your Programme.

Programme Planning

Overview of the Balanced Programme

The Programme Zones

The Methods

Balanced Programme Checker

Programme Planning

Term Planning

Term Plan

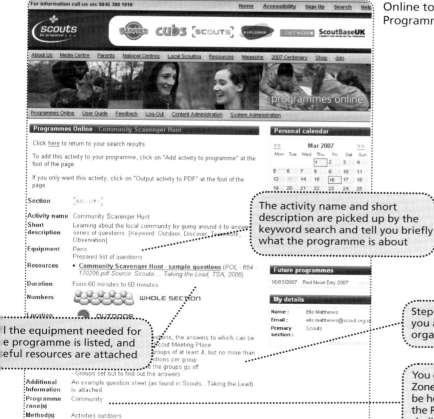

POL SEE ALSO NEXT PAGE →

SCAVENGER HUNT EXAMPLE

In your teams, find the answers to the following questions.

1.	The website address for The Scout Association	
2.	The number of lamp posts in Clifton Road	
3.	The time that the first 79 bus (heading towards Edgeware) arrives at Iceland	
4.	The price of a litre of unleaded petrol at the Total petrol station	
5.	The telephone number of the public phone box in Kenton Road	
6.	The monarch in whose reign the post box in Shrewsbury Avenue was errected	
7.	The name of the Headteacher at Glebe Middle School	
8.	The width of the width restriction in Charlton Road	
9.	How many bungalows in Winchester Road?	
10.	The name of the firm of accountants on the corner of Winckley Close	
11.	The name of the church in Loretto Gardens	
12.	What army units meet at the TA Centre in Honeyport Lane?	
13.	The time of the last post on Saturdays from the pillar box in St. Paul's Avenue	

Please ensure that you return to the Scout headquarters within 1 hour.

> Resources can be photocopied as they are, or adapted for local use.

> The good thing about this is that you don't have to spend ages creating your own resources, and you can be reassured that this programme has been run by an experienced Leader before.

The companion volume, *The Troop Programme Plus (volumes one and two)* shows some of the ideas in Programmes Online as well as offering further ideas, games, activities and skill instructions.

The Troop Forum also provides an ideal source of programme ideas. Don't worry if you haven't got the skills or knowledge to run an activity that you or your Scouts want to do. Ask around in your District and County or Area and you will be sure to find someone who does.

Finally, add the Challenges and the Activity Badges that the Scout want to do, to the list of programme ideas.

Step 3 – Review last year's Troop programme

Using 'Programme-Review' (see *Troop Essentials*) can help you see how well you did last year. You may find that there are Challenges and Activity Badges to revisit and Programme Zones and Methods that need to be emphasised. The Balanced Programme Checker is another tool to help you review your programmes (See page 10). All these details should go on your list.

Step 4 – Decide on activities

Once you have the main points plotted on your calendar, you can start filling in some of the other details. The competition hike in April will require some preparation for walking and navigation. The canoe trip in June will need Scouts to at least paddle in a straight line. You will therefore need to plot some time at the local water activity base and possibly a visit to a local pool. There will also be camps during the year. Some might be just overnight, others a weekend, others for a longer period, such as a summer camp. How will you need to prepare your Scouts to take part?

Step 5 – Publicise your activities and events

As your programme starts to take shape, get the dates into print and out to your Scouts so that families know what is on offer, and can plan their diaries. It is a good idea to indicate at this stage who the activities are targeted at and the likely cost. For example, if you plan to take your older Scouts karting in April, be clear about the lower age limit so that younger Scouts are not disappointed nearer the time.

Step 6 – Organise Leaders, Assistants and other adults

Keep a note of who is organising each event on your list. This can then be updated and revised at your regular Leader meetings.

PROGRAMME PLANNING

This is an extract from a four month (or a term) section of an annual overview.

Term Overview

	September	October	November	December
SAT				
SUN	1			1
MON	2			2
TUE	3 Schools go back	1		3
WED	4 Fit for Life	2 Community/Beliefs and Attitudes		4 Global
THU	5	3		5
FRI	6	4	1	6
SAT	7	5 District Camp	2 District Swimming Gala	7
SUN	8	6	3	8
MON	9	7	4	9
TUE	10	8	5	10
WED	11 Outdoor and Adventure	9 Outdoor and Adventure	6 Outdoor and Adventure	11 Creative Expression
THU	12	10	7	12
FRI	13	11	8	13
SAT	14 Patrol Camps	12	9 Diwali	14 Eid-ul-Adha
SUN	15 Patrol Camps	13	10 Remembrance Service at War Memorial	15 Carol Service
MON	16	14	11	16
TUE	17	15	12	17
WED	18 Creative Expression/ Investitures	16 Global	13 Outdoor and Adventure	18 Last meeting/ Party - Community
THU	19	17	14	19
FRI	20	18	15	20
SAT	21 District Orienteering	19	16	21
SUN	22	20	17 County Hike	22
MON	23	21	18	23
TUE	24	22 Half Term	19	24 Christmas Break
WED	25 Outdoor and Adventure	23 No meeting	20 Creative Expression	25
THU	26	24 County Gang Show	21	26
FRI	27	25 County Gang Show	22	27
SAT	28	26 County Gang Show	23	28
SUN	29	27	24	29
MON	30	28	25	30
TUE		29	26	31
WED		30 Fit for Life	27 Community	
THU		31	28	
FRI			29	
SAT			30	

Key

WED	- Troop meeting
MON	- School holiday/ Days off
SAT	- District/County events

TERM PLANNING

The term overview plan takes a block of 12 to 16 weeks (about a term) of your annual overview and increases the level of detail. It identifies which activities are to be done week by week. As in the annual overview, there is no particular order in which the first three steps need to be done.

Step 1 – Review and update your annual overview

At this stage add any new dates and information that may have become available and confirm your commitment to the activities already identified. Don't forget to check the availability of your adult Leaders and Assistants.

Step 2 – Gather further ideas

Your annual overview may have identified what your Scouts want to do but not how to do it. You may therefore be looking for some more ways of delivering the Programme. Always keep your eyes and ears open for new opportunities. If your Troop has an opportunity to try dragon boat racing, don't pass this up simply because the activity was not part of your original plan.

Ask your own Scouts for their thoughts, through the Troop Forum.

Step 3 – Review the Troop programme over the last few months

Be particularly aware of any Programme Zones or Methods that do not play a big part in your programme. You might also want to consider the time that has been committed to the programme over this period and the distribution of tasks among the leadership team.

Step 4 – Decide on the programme for the period

When you are deciding on your term programme plan, you need to include the camps, activities and competitions, the Challenges and the Activity Badges, together with the skill training and preparation needed. Not all of the programme can be delivered at Troop night and during camps. You will find that your programme may also need your Scouts' time on other evenings and weekends. It is important that you and your team keep a realistic view of how much of your time you have available to commit to running your Troop.

The programme should also include the theme for your Troop meeting. At this stage, check that the programme is taking shape and is drawing ideas from all the Programme Zones.

Step 5 – Book facilities and publicise activities and events

Now you have a clearer idea of the activities you are doing, it may be time to start booking facilities. You will also need to confirm that your plans do not clash with other Sections. The Cub Scout Pack may, for example, have already booked the tents for the camp you wanted to organise. They may also have the minibus as well!

Arrange to send information out to Scouts and their families. Do not forget that one of the ways to ensure that you get a good response is to give Scouts and their parents and carers as much notice as possible.

Balanced Programme Checker for a term - showing that all the Programme Zones have been touched - with a good spread of methods.

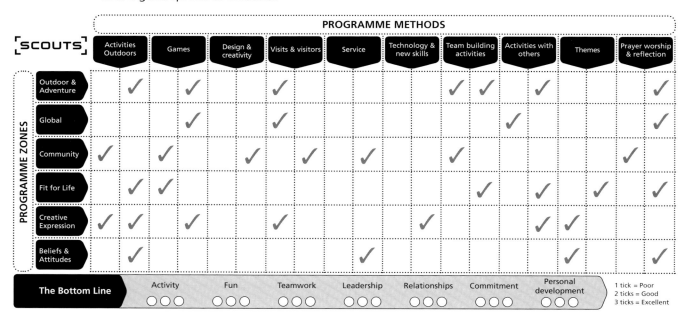

TERM PLAN

October: Term planning

	Wednesday	Thursday	Friday	Saturday	Sunday	Monday	Tuesday
	2 Troop Night (Community/Beliefs and Attitudes) Potato Day in France • visit to Clive's allotment to learn about vegetable growing and help on the plot. Reflection (food-themed). – Sue	3	4 Preparation for District Camp Patrol Leaders help Hugh with tents. Mike to organise food shop. Pack van.	5 District Camp Highvale Campsite activities start at 12.00pm.	6 Return from Camp parents picking up at 5.00pm	7	8
	9 Troop Night Outdoor and Adventure • Tent-pitching outside with Outdoor Challenge Scouts. Sue to lead navigation exercise with others. Play Danish Schlurp game.	10	11 Patrol Leaders Forum 6.00 pm to discuss activity for next Troop meeting and team for Swimming Gala. Also check equipment.	12	13	14	15
	16 Global Black History Month Activities from the internet • Patrol Leaders to organise one activity. Play Mancala game.	17	18	19	20	21	22
	23	24 County Gang Show Lowtown Festival Hall 7.15pm • Selling programmes at Theatre • full smart uniform required.	25 County Gang Show	26 County Gang Show NOTE: Clocks go back	27	28	29 Remind Scouts to bring bikes tomorrow.
	30 Fit for Life BMX rally inter Patrol contest meet early to get to Bike track for 6.30 bring torch/flashlights.						

November: Term planning

	Wednesday	Thursday	Friday	Saturday	Sunday
			1	2 District Swimming Gala • Lowtown Pool (3.00pm) • Two teams Hugh, Sue and Explorer Leaders.	3
	6 Troop Night Outdoor and Adventure	7	8	9 Diwali • Trip to London for Scouts doing World Faiths badge • 8.00am leave HQ, return 7.00pm	10 Remembrance Service at War Memorial Need one Scout for a reading, full smart uniform.
	13 Global Activities from the internet • Patrol Leaders to organise one activity.	14	15	16	17 County Hike (25km) Minibus leaves HQ at 6.45am • Mike and Sue. Hugh on organising team.
	20 Troop night Creative Expression Ready Steady Cook night • Patrol Leaders to arrive early for briefing. Sue.	21	22	23	24
	27 Troop night Community Make bird feeders and hang in trees locally. Hugh and Patrol Leaders.	28	29	30 St Andrew's Day Maintenance Day at HQ (Parents and Scouts invited) • Scottish treats during the day • Use for DIY badge.	

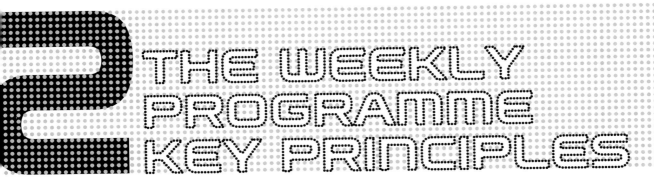

2 THE WEEKLY PROGRAMME KEY PRINCIPLES

EVERY WEEK, OVER 6,500 SCOUT MEETINGS ARE ORGANISED THROUGHOUT THE UK. THESE MEETINGS HOLD THE LIFE OF THE TROOP TOGETHER. IT IS THROUGH THEM THAT SCOUTS ENJOY THE COMPANY OF OTHERS AND GROW AND DEVELOP THROUGH THEIR INVOLVEMENT IN THE BALANCED PROGRAMME.

Because many young people have busy lives, it is important that most Troop meetings start and finish at a set time and place each week. However, apart from this consideration, the programme should be as varied as possible from week to week. An occasional change of time or place will help to spark some extra interest, but do not put too many strains on parents and carers, who have their own commitments and may also have to organise other young people.

TROOP MEETINGS

The organisation of Troop meetings will be influenced by a number of factors, not least the venue. When Scouts Groups have their own Meeting Place, each Section may have their own meeting night. This means that while the Troop meeting may run from 7.15pm to 9.00pm, there is still plenty of additional time before and after the meeting to prepare, set up equipment and meet with Leaders, parents and carers.

Troops that have the use of a school or local hall may have to organise the meeting for the Beaver Scout, Cub Scout and Scout Sections all on one night. This will obviously affect what can be done in the hall. There will be very little time available to set up before the meeting and to clear away afterwards.

Even if you have your own building in which to meet, having regular outdoor meetings is also very important. Although factors such as transport, safety and weather will increase the need for pre-meeting planning, the extra effort is well worth making. Having regular Troop meetings in familiar outdoor settings will allow you and your Troop to develop an organised routine for these meetings.

Troop meetings can take many forms and there is no set way of running a meeting. Some meetings will involve a mix of games, training and activities. Some meetings will be made up of one long activity and some may involve groups of Scouts being at different locations. Traditionally, a Troop meeting will involve a flag break, a short prayer and inspection, with flag down and prayer at the end. However, there is no obligation to repeat this format every week. A good meeting programme should reflect some distinct characteristics:

- **Variety**

The Troop night programme must be different from what your Scouts do at school or other youth clubs and from what they did at last week's meeting.

- **Participation**

The programme will need to involve some watching and some listening, but mostly should involve taking part. Learning by doing has always been the most effective way for Scouts to learn. Make sure everyone is involved, including Leaders, Assistants and Scouts, for most of the time during the evening.

- **Balance**

The programme must be drawn from all the Programme Zones using a range of different Methods. Many of the Zones can be explored further by using the Challenges and the Activity Badges.

The number of adults and young people involved will also influence the programme. A Troop meeting for 36 Scouts and half a dozen adults will not be the same as a meeting of nine Scouts and two Leaders. The spread of ages across the Troop will also be a factor, as is the willingness and ability of the older Scouts to help train and lead the younger Scouts.

Before the meeting

Once the detailed programme for the week has been produced, there will still be a number of jobs to do. The list below will help you consider some of these tasks and which members of your team might take responsibility.

- Prepare any equipment or materials needed for each game and activity.

- Buy any extra equipment that you may need.

- Brief any visitors who might be coming specifically to run an activity.

- Complete a Risk Assessment, particularly for any activity you have not done before. Check you are complying with any special activity rules, by checking in *Policy, Organisation and Rules* (POR). More information about Risk Assessments can be found in *Troop Essentials*.

- Check your First Aid kit is adequately stocked. The factsheet *First Aid Kits and Activity Books* (FS140048) can be obtained from www.scouts.org.uk/factsheets

- Produce any letter or other information about forthcoming activities, which parents and carers may need.

During the meeting

- Make sure that all your Leaders and Scouts are fully involved in the meeting.

- Make sure that there is enough supervision at all times. This is especially important during the time before the start of the meeting, when the Scouts first arrive.

- Be flexible. If a new game is not working, or is going really well, adjust the programme accordingly.

- Enjoy it!

After the meeting

- Thank all those who have contributed in any way to the meeting.

- Keep a note of any money that has been given to you and make sure it is recorded in the Troop or Group account and banked as soon as possible.

- Do a quick review of the meeting. Did the programme run to time? Did all the activities hold the Scouts' attention? What improvements could have been made?

- File a copy of the meeting programme together with any notes you have made during your review and any Risk Assessment you may have done.

EMERGENCY PROGRAMMES

It is always a good idea to have a few ideas that you can introduce into the programme at a moment's notice. You may need them when something unexpected happens, for example, some of your Leaders may be delayed at work, or an activity that you thought would take 40 minutes finishes in half the time. Your reserve programme ideas should not be complicated and need very little time to set up.

Basic programme equipment

- Beanbags: three or four per Patrol
- Collection of 2m length cords: ideally, enough for one per Scout
- Two large sponge balls for indoor use
- Two plastic footballs for outside use
- Pencils: one for each Scout
- Two pencil sharpeners
- Newspaper: one per Patrol
- Plain paper: ream of copy paper or out-of-date company headed paper
- Ruler or other measure: one per Patrol
- 10 x 30cm high plastic bollards
- Scissors for paper: one per Patrol
- Box of chalk
- Ordnance Survey 1:50 000 Maps: one per Patrol
- Felt-tip marker
- Assorted quizzes and puzzles from books and magazines
- Box of trivia questions

EMERGENCY IDEAS

Games are a good standby activity, and it is worth noting which games work best for you and your Troop.

Here are some other activity ideas:

Judge a minute

Each Scout puts their hand over their watch, and then walks around the room. Walking around makes it slightly harder to judge the passing of time. When they think one minute has passed, they sit down. Who is the most accurate?

Pin point

Each group of Scouts takes the grid reference of six letters from place names on their map. They have five minutes to do this. They then pass the map and the grid references to another Patrol, who locate the letters, and then make as many five-letter words as they can.

Trivia quiz

Sit the Scouts down in relay formation. At the far end of the hall, have an A4 sheet for each Patrol, with the word TRUE written on one side and FALSE written on the other. When you ask a question, the next Scout in each Patrol runs to the far end of the hall and holds up the appropriate answer.

Alternatively, each team sits behind their table. Ask team one a question. If they get it right, you ask them another. Each Patrol can be asked up to four questions. If they get an answer wrong, it passes to the next team. If the other team answers correctly, the next set of questions moves to them, and they have the opportunity to answer four questions.

Skill challenge

Organise a number of skill bases, which the Scouts visit in turn.

1. Limbo dancing under a pole. Who can go the lowest?

2. Shuttle runs between the two points, picking up one beanbag each time. Who is the fastest?

3. Dribbling a football around a course marked by bollards. Who is the most skilful?

4. Sitting on a chair and throwing a ball backwards over your head. Who can throw the furthest?

Paper plane

Build a number of paper darts of different sizes and see which flies the furthest, highest or for longest.

Through the middle

Give each group a sheet of newspaper and a pair of scissors, and challenge the Scouts to cut a hole large enough for each member of the group to pass through.

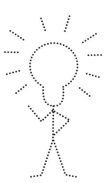

3 TROOP NIGHT PROGRAMMES IN DETAIL

TROOP NIGHTS CAN TAKE MANY FORMS, BUT CAN BE BROKEN DOWN INTO SIX MAIN TYPES. YOU DON'T HAVE TO KEEP THEM AS SEPARATE TYPES. USE THEM IN ANY WAY THAT YOU WANT.

The six main types of Programme a Troop might have:

- **Traditional programmes**
- **Matrix**
- **Half matrix**
- **Challenge/project/competitive/scavenger hunt**
- **Games night**
- **Theme night**
- **Visits**

TRADITIONAL PROGRAMMES

The traditional approach to Troop night divides the evening into a number of stages. Some Troops like to run a 'coming in game' to involve all the Scouts as they gather for the meeting. Other Troops prefer for the Scouts to make their own entertainment. They often use the time to catch up on news, speak to their Patrol Leader or Scout Leader and hand in any money or application forms.

Opening routine

There is no one correct way of doing any of the following parts of the opening routine, but over time different Troops have developed different traditions. This is the formal gathering of the Troop, bringing everyone together. You can create healthy inter-Patrol rivalry by insisting that all Scouts fall in quickly once the instruction has been given and praising the Patrol who does so fastest.

Fall in and Flag break

Troops form up at the start of Troop night in different ways, although most make a semicircle or horseshoe of which each Patrol forms a part. Sea Scout Troops divide the Patrols into watches and form up in straight lines. Those who use the Union flag will have attached it to a high point such as a mast or a pulley in the ceiling. At the correct time, one Scout will step forward, tug at the cord and the flag will 'break' (unfurl).

The Scout then takes a step back, salutes, and the rest of the Troop salute at the same time. The Sea Scouting tradition is again rather different. Sea Scouts do not break the flag from the top of the pole but 'run' it slowly up the mast.

Prayer

Prayer, worship and reflection is one of the Methods for delivering the Programme. There are many books available with short prayers and reflections for young people, but perhaps the most effective are those written by the Scouts themselves. Remember, several faiths may be represented in your Troop.

Inspection

Scouting is a values-based organisation. How we dress, is in some ways, a sign of our values. We need to encourage the Scouts to take pride in who they are and in what they wear. An inspection at the start of the meeting is a chance to check that the uniform is complete and badges are correctly displayed. While some Troops may do a full inspection every week, others may check just one or two items at random. For example, scarves and woggles one week, badges on the left sleeve the next. You can award more points to Scouts or Patrols who have made an effort than to those who have not.

Game

The first game is the incentive to get through the opening procedures with the maximum amount of co-operation and the minimum amount of time wasting. It should involve everyone.

Activities and training

This is the opportunity for some training or other structured activity. Many of the events that the Scouts will take part in both at and away from Troop night will call for knowledge and skills. This part of the meeting can be used to help Scouts gain those skills. For example, before going to camp, a Scout should be able to find and pack personal kit, be able to help pitch a tent, or know how to light a fire or stove. For all the activities your Scouts may take part in, from archery to youth hostelling, time spent in preparation and learning the background skills will be time well spent. It is also worth considering how the Troop is divided up, as not all the Scouts will want to be doing the same activities at the same time. The older Scouts will certainly want to feel they are making progress. You can, of course, arrange for some of the Patrol Leaders and other older Scouts to pass on their skills to the younger Scouts in the time-honoured tradition.

Second game

A second quick game will bring the Troop back together again after the training and activity exercises.

Contest or competition

This is a further opportunity for some inter-Patrol rivalry and gives the older Scouts and Patrol Leaders the chance to practice their leadership and people management skills. The activity could build on and test skills that have been learnt earlier in the evening, or it can be just for fun!

Closing sequence

Notices

A Troop with a busy programme will have to give out a lot of paperwork to keep Scouts, parents and carers informed about forthcoming events. There are dates for the diary, initial information sheets about camps or other events, health and general consent forms, camp kit lists, final arrangements and reminders about jumble sales or the AGM. This is all part of good communication practice. Make sure that when you plan the programme, you include enough time to give out notices. Parents and carers do not like to be kept waiting outside because the meeting is over-running.

Be wary when giving Scouts things to take home. An important letter often gets folded up and lost in a pocket and not discovered until the trousers are washed! A useful tip is to bulk purchase clear plastic wallets and get the Scouts to take all messages home in one of these. You might also like to consider the use of email and your own website. For more information on good communications, see *Troop Essentials*.

Flag down

If you broke or raised the flag at the start of the meeting, you need to bring the flag down at the end. This should again be done smartly and respectfully, but this time without the Salute. The flag should come down slowly and should not be allowed to touch the floor. It is worth rehearsing this with your Scouts so that it does not become a laughing matter, but a meaningful ceremony at the end of another good Scout meeting.

Prayer

As at the opening, this is another chance to pause and reflect. Give Scouts the opportunity to write their own prayers, which can then be bound together so that you have a folder full of good material to select at the appropriate time.

TRADITIONAL TROOP MEETING PROGRAMME

The following is an example of a traditional Troop meeting:

Time	Activity	Resources needed	Run by
7.00	Leaders' briefing		John
7.15	Coming in game (Cat and Mouse)		Sue
7.30	Fall In (Points Awarded for the first Patrol) Welcome Flag break (Reflection/prayer) Inspection (Left arm of shirt)	Use Troop Prayer file	Duty Patrol Leader John Team
7.40	Game One: Quads		John
8.00	Group A Knotting Group B Codes Group C Navigation and map Quiz	Ropes and spars	John Sue Senior Patrol Leader
8.30	Bucket ball	Benches and two buckets	Sue
8.45	Inter Patrol Activity Build a Pharaoh's Chariot		All
9.00	Inter Patrol Chariot Race		All
9.10	Tidy up and clear away		
9.15	Fall in Notices (see Leader file) Flag down and reflection Dismissal and good night		Senior Patrol Leader John & Sue

This is how it looks on the Balanced Programme Checker:

Balanced Programme Checker for a month (or 3 group meetings)

Meeting notes

Troop Night Programmes

Traditional Programmes

⊹ Traditional Troop Meeting Programme

Matrix Meetings

Challenge /Project/ Competition/Scavenger Hunt

Scavenger Hunt

World Fair Challenge

Incident Hike Programme

Games Nights

Theme Nights

Visits

Activity	How to do it	Kit needed
Cat & Mouse (Coming in game).	Scouts stand around the playing area in pairs. One Scout is the cat, and another the mouse. The cat chases the mouse around the area of play. At any point, the mouse can stop and stand alongside any other pair, and immediately the Scout at the other end becomes the mouse, which the cat has to chase. If the cat catches the mouse, their roles are reversed.	none
Quads	Divide your Meeting Place into four adjacent zones of equal size. • Divide the Section into four teams with an equal number of players in each team • The aim of the game is to keep the ball out of your team's zone. Scouts have no idea how long the round will last. A Leader – hidden from view – blows a whistle at random intervals. All teams start with five points, and lose a point if the ball is in their quad when the whistle blows. • Players are only allowed to hit the ball with their hands and must not hold onto the ball and then wait for the game to end	Rope of tape to divide the hall into four. One or more balls
Basic knotting	Two knots are covered, the clove hitch and the round turn and two half hitches – both of which are needed for the later game.	Ropes, poles or staves
Codes	Scouts learn some simple codes that can be used to disguise their messages. Challenge them to decode each other's messages.	Sample codes
Navigation & Map Quiz	Scouts check out their knowledge of map work, by completing a simple quiz based on a local OS map, e.g. What river flows through Royham? Which A-road links Cheswick with Faraday? What is the hill above Piton Village known as?	OS maps and quiz questions.
Bucket Bench Ball	Place a bench at each end of the playing area with two equal teams • One team member stands on the bench at the opposite end to the rest of their team, holding a bucket. • Players cannot move when holding the ball. • The object is to get ball into the bucket held by their team mate on the bench. • After each goal, the person on the scoring bench changes.	Two benches, two buckets and a ball
Pharaoh's Chariot	Give each team three staves or light pioneering poles and three lashing lengths about three metres long. • Find the middle of each lashing length, and at that point tie a clove hitch around the centre pole; one should be tied at the centre of the pole, the other two approximately 30cm (a ruler length in from each end) • Keeping the distance between the poles correct, tie one end of each lashing length to each outer pole, using a round turn and two half hitches. • The smallest member of each group should be the first rider; everyone else becomes a carrier, with at least two young people on each outer pole. • The rider stands astride the central pioneering pole, just behind the centre knot, holding the other two poles, which should be at waste height. • The carriers lift the outer poles, so that the rope goes taut but the centre pole remains on the ground, and holds them about one metre apart. The course can include a few simple obstacles. Swap around, so that everyone has a go.	Scout staves (or broom sticks) Lashing ropes. Instructions for the activity can be written in code.

The main part of the meeting revolves around the Outdoors and Adventure Zone with the two sessions on rope work and navigation. The team games and the Pharaoh's Chair helped develop team building, and contribute to both the Fit for Life Zone and possibly some Design and Creativity. The use of codes both as a session and in the chariot race also introduces a creative element. The prayers or reflections and the start and finish of the evening provide a contribution from the Beliefs and Attitude Zone.

MATRIX MEETINGS

Matrix meetings are built around the principle that Scouts will be prepared to do almost anything for ten minutes. It keeps them in small Patrols or friendship teams. Smaller groups are also much less daunting for your Assistant Leaders to work with. The Scouts quickly become familiar with the format but the content is always different! The more Scouts you have in the Troop, the larger the matrix. Anything that can be done with four to six Scouts in ten minutes can be fitted into a matrix. It provides a good opportunity to pass on many skills and techniques that can be tested and developed later. It is also a very effective way of providing short activities to cover all the Programme Zones.

If you are running a matrix meeting, one of the ten minute slots can be given over to the notices. You can spend more time explaining forthcoming events than you can with the whole Troop at the end of the evening. You can also individually encourage Scouts to take part.

Sample matrix meeting for three groups

Time	Activity	Kit needed	Run by
7.40	Game: Uni-hoc. Two teams, number up, call out numbers, those called run to pick up the stick and try to score a goal at opposite ends of the meeting place. Play until everyone has had at least one go, until there is a winner.	Uni-hoc sticks, tennis ball, benches for goals.	Jane
7.55	Matrix Activity Briefing	Leaders set up their activity at this point	Alex
	Foxes	Wolves	Bulldogs
8.00	Mini-pioneering (main hall).	Sheepdog trials (outside).	Refugees and Asylum Seekers (Patrol Leaders' Den)
8.16	Refugees and Asylum Seekers (PLs' Den)	Mini-pioneering (main hall).	Sheepdog trials (outside).
8.32	Sheepdog trials (outside).	Refugees and Asylum Seekers (PLs' Den)	Mini-pioneering (main hall).
8.50	Fall-in/Notices/Reflection (Marcus has prepared this for his Promise Challenge).		

Meeting notes

Mini-pioneering	Making towers and bridges out of spaghetti and blu-tac. The idea is to create a mini settlement with everyone's contributions. Kit needed - spaghetti packets, blu-tac (or marshmallows), scissors. Run by Dev.
Sheepdog Trials	One Patrol member is the sheepdog/shepherd; the others are the sheep. The Patrol has two minutes to decide on signals for different directions using a whistle. They then have the remaining time to navigate a marked out course, ending up in the pen. Kit needed - Cones, rope, whistle. Run by Chris.
Refugees and Asylum Seekers	Visit from local refugee project worker, talk about asylum issues and do some activities about asylum/refugees. Kit needed - TV/video.

Sample matrix meeting for four groups

Time	Activity	Kit needed	Run by
7.40	Game: Chair Relay. Random groups of five. Each group has four chairs. Race to get whole team to marked line and back, without touching the floor.	Four chairs per group.	Hugh
7.55	Matrix Activity Briefing	Leaders set up their activity at this point	Alex

Time	Outdoor Challenge Group	Investiture Group	Fitness Challenge Group	Patrol Leaders
8.00	Packing a rucksack	Law and Promise	Watch 100 Years of Scouting DVD	Planning for next week's Patrol Leaders' meeting
8.12	Circus Skills - Juggling (scarves, rings and balls)		Medley relay (outside).	
8.24	Trangia stoves	Watch 100 Years of Scouting DVD	Showing/updating fitness logs - week 3	Ideas for Summer camp theme/activities
8.36	Trangia stoves	Watch 100 Years of Scouting DVD	Showing/updating fitness logs - week 3	Ideas for Summer camp theme/activities
8.36	Watch 100 Years of Scouting DVD	Scout Motto, Scout Sign, Salute and Handshake	Watch 100 Years of Scouting DVD	
8.48	Medley Relay (outside).		Practice fitness activity	Watch 100 Years of Scouting DVD
9.00	Fall-in/Flag down/reflection/fall out			

Meeting notes

Outdoor Challenge	
	Scouts in this group: Meena, Jack, Ally, Bryn, Alexander
Packing a rucksack	Basic principles of packing for camp. Where to put light/heavy, lining the rucksack. Use factsheet.
Trangia Stoves	Explain how to light, extinguish, safety aspects, boil a pot of tea with one stove during session.
Investiture group	**Alex to lead**
	Scouts in this group: Tom, Farid, Sandy, Stephen
Law and Promise	Explain the meaning of the Promise and have a discussion about the Scout Law and how it is relevant to them in their daily lives.
Scout Motto, Scout Sign, Salute and Handshake	Tell the story of B-P, Dinizulu, and how the left handshake came to be part of Scouting. Explain the Motto, Sign and Salute. Allow a few minutes to practice these ready for the Investiture.
Fitness Challenge	**Susan to lead**
	Scouts in this group: Andrew, Marvin, Jade, Holly, Jessica, Greg, Duncan
Update logs	Check what has been done in the last two weeks, make sure there is enough written; give advice on what to do next week.
Practice fitness activity	To include appropriate warm-up. Equipment may be needed.
Joint activities	**Susan to lead**
Medley relay	Young Leaders to lead, supervised by Hugh.
Four legs	1 – Run backwards • 2 – Sack race • 3 – Wheelbarrow • 4 – Sprint. Teams of four will need someone to double up on the wheelbarrow leg. Kit needed – cones and sacks.
Circus Skills	Visit from members of the circus visiting town. Ten minutes on basics of juggling. Equipment will be provided by guests.
Watch 100 Years of Scouting DVD	

Balanced Programme Checker for the sample programme for four groups

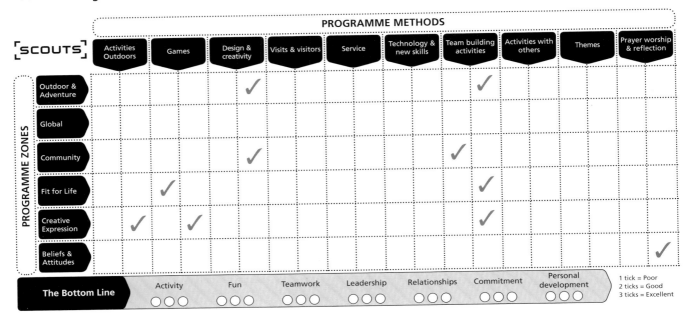

HALF MATRIX

This style of meeting allows the Troop to be split to make the best use of the resources available. Some members of the Troop are involved in an activity taking a longer period of time, while others take part in a series of short sessions.

Half matrix meeting programme

Structure

- Time intervals consistent again
- Four teams
- Split programme in half, with one activity taking up half the programme time
- Split the other half into four short activities

Sample half matrix meeting for four groups

Time	Activity			
7.40	5 minute activity briefing			
	Team A	Team B	Team C	Team D
7.45	Orienteering training for District Orienteering Competition		Scouting Skills	Community
7.56			Creative 1	Creative 2
8.07	Meet outside HQ		Community	Scouting Skills
8.18			Creative 2	Creative
8.30	Drinks Break			
8.40	Scouting Skills	Community	Orienteering training for District Orienteering Competition	
8.51	Creative 1	Creative 2		
9.02	Community	Scouting Skills	Meet outside HQ	
9.13	Creative 2	Creative 1		
9.25	Fall-in, notices and flag down			

Meeting notes

Scouting Skills - Square lashings	Patrol Leaders teach square lashing to those in Patrol that don't know it. Patrol build simple A-frame with three lashings. Explain these will be tested next week. Kit - pioneering poles, lashing rope, knot encyclopaedia.
Creative 1 - Write a song/poem/rap about the recent Patrol camp	Explain these will be performed at the start of next week's meeting, so they should each write down a copy of the lyrics and learn them. Kit - pencils, paper, musical instruments box.
Community - Make a page for the Guest Guide Book being made for the Italian Scouts who are visiting in the summer	This could include useful local information, but should be graphic, colourful. Kit - yellow pages, OS Maps, council leaflets, coloured pens, paper, laptop.
Creative 2 - 3D Noughts and Crosses	Pair up and play 3D noughts-and-crosses, best of three to determine the Patrol champion. Kit - 3D Noughts and Crosses boards and pieces.

Balanced Programme Checker for sample matrix meeting for four groups

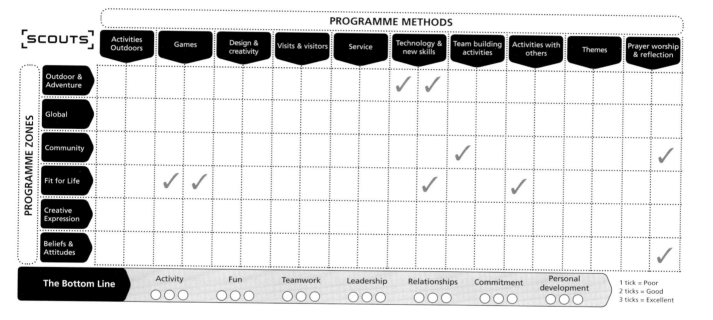

CHALLENGE/PROJECT/ COMPETITION/SCAVENGER HUNT

These meetings encourage Scouts to organise themselves to achieve a number of challenges and goals during the course of a given period. The challenge may or may not take up the full meeting and they can take any number of formats, including incident hikes.

Whenever possible, the event should have a competitive edge. Having said that, all Scouts should be congratulated at the end for the contribution they have made to the Patrol or team effort. Although winning is important, so too is taking part. There are valuable lessons to be learned from being part of a team. It is important that all are encouraged to complete their challenge and not just to give up because somebody else has completed theirs first.

The challenge could include:

- something that requires building, making or creating

- information that needs to be collected

- tasks that need to be achieved

- places that need to be visited

- puzzles that need to be solved.

Sometimes the challenges may include more than can be achieved in the time. Teams or Patrols need to make decisions about what they can and can't do in the time available.

SCAVENGER HUNT

This game requires some more preparation. Not all the information can be found by just walking up the High Street, so the team will need to plan how they are going to find the information. They will need to visit a library, or go to the home of a Scout who lives nearby with Internet access. There is also a creative element and the efforts of the team will need to be coordinated by the Patrol Leader.

Scavenger hunt 1

This involves the Scouts going out into the local shopping area and finding out information. This scavenger hunt was run in North London, and is only a sample of more than 30 questions that were asked. You should visit the location the day before to set the questions. Rounding off the game with the teams ringing an answerphone for their final instructions adds an extra twist. This might direct them to the local fish and chip shop where they will be provided with a free bag of chips to share on the way back to the Meeting Place.

SCAVENGER HUNT

Priority: Read this first.

- Keep together as a Group. Do not let anyone become separated.

- Keep an eye on the time. Make sure you all return by 9.00pm.

- Take care when crossing any roads. Motorists may not expect young people out at this time of night.

- Show respect for other people. They know you are Scouts.

Question	Your answer
1. Which two stores in the high street use the same alarm system?	
2. What is the caretaker's name at Middleton Primary School?	
3. Who is the new hair stylist in 'Top Cut'?	
4. What is the name of the dog that has been lost? (See the poster on the tree).	
5. What is the time of the last collection from the letterbox outside the butchers?	
6. What is the cost of a double cheeseburger in the burger bar?	
7. What buses stop at the bus stop outside the pub?	
8. Before it became a nursery, what was the building now used by Tiny Tots originally used for?	
9. How much is an eye test in the opticians?	
10. Telephone 020 8123 1234, listen to the message – and complete the task.	

Scavenger hunt 2

This game requires less preparation as the information required is not as time sensitive as in the earlier game. Not all the information would be found simply by visiting the High Street, so the teams will need to plan how best to find the answers. They may need to visit a library, or go to the home of the nearest Scout to get 'online'. There is clearly a creative element to the game and the efforts of the team will need to be co-ordinated by the Patrol Leader.

SCAVENGER HUNT 2

Priority: Read this first.

- You have just one hour to get yourselves organised and complete as many of the following as you can.
- You will need to manage your time and your resources well. (At no time must fewer than three Scouts be in a group).
- Take account of which questions are the most valuable.
- Exercise great care when crossing roads
- Be back at Meeting Place by 9.10pm.

Question	Worth	Your answer
1. How many roads in the town have 'Green' in the title?	10	
2. What do we mean by 'Pandora's Box'?	20	
3. How would you get from Restley to Abbotsvale by bus?	10	
4. What is the most expensive meal at the Indian restaurant?	10	
5. Make up a limerick and recite it with each Scout taking a line in turn.	20	
6. What is a Compression Capnut and who would use one?	20	
7. Prove you have all stood next to the letterbox in George Street	10	

Be clear about the time the Scout should return. It is useful to have a couple of mobile numbers for each team taking part and to provide each team with an emergency number that they can ring, should they have a problem. All activities of this nature need to be risk assessed before the Scouts take part (see chapter 5 of *Troop Essentials*).

PROGRAMME METHODS

SCOUTS	Activities Outdoors	Games	Design & creativity	Visits & visitors	Service	Technology & new skills	Team building activities	Activities with others	Themes	Prayer worship & reflection
Outdoor & Adventure		✓					✓			
Global										
Community	✓	✓	✓	✓			✓			
Fit for Life										
Creative Expression	✓						✓			
Beliefs & Attitudes										

PROGRAMME ZONES

The Bottom Line	Activity	Fun	Teamwork	Leadership	Relationships	Commitment	Personal development
	○○○	○○○	○○○	○○○	○○○	○○○	○○○

1 tick = Poor
2 ticks = Good
3 ticks = Excellent

Programme Checker

The Scavenger hunt links with three Programme Zones, and in the Community Zone particularly, it uses four methods: Activities outdoors, Games, Design and creativity and Team building.

TEAM CHALLENGE

The team challenge is focused on producing or making something, in this case a camp gadget for a World Fair. However, the team also has to manage a number of other activities, which can be anything from contributing a handprint to a Troop collage to teaching younger Scouts from another Patrol the Water Safety Code.

World Fair Challenge

Team name: [   ]

Your Patrol has been invited to represent Scouting at a World Fair to be held at 8.45pm, this evening. You must complete all the requirements, and be prepared and on time for the exhibition in full uniform.

Challenge	Points gained
Using whatever you can find in the equipment stores, build a camp gadget that you can showcase at the World Fair, with a full demonstration.	
Write a press release about your invention. It must use the words 'phenomenon' and 'enormous'.	
As a maintenance task, every 10 minutes provide one person from the team, who must report to Hugh.	
Devise a jingle to advertise your invention. Be prepared to perform it at the World Fair.	
In which year was the Great Exhibition held at Hyde Park in a Crystal Palace?	
Take part in the World Fair.	

INCIDENT HIKE PROGRAMME

These can provide a half-day's activity at camp, but can be shortened to provide an activity for a Troop night. The incidents that are included on the hike will depend on the environment you have available within a short distance of your meeting place.

Don't forget to prepare for what happens if Scouts get lost. How would a Patrol contact you if they had a problem? Do you need some older Scouts, or Explorer Scouts patrolling the area on bikes?

Incident 1 – Towers of Hanoi

Set up the problem with tyres and posts hammered into the ground. The challenge is to move the five different sized tyres from the 'start' to the 'finish position' in as few moves as possible.

It takes a minimum of 31 moves to complete this challenge. To find the full answer, go to Programmes Online (www.scouts.org.uk/pol) and search for 'Towers of Hanoi'.

Doing the activity for real will mean the incident is in both the Fit for Life and Creative Expression Zones!

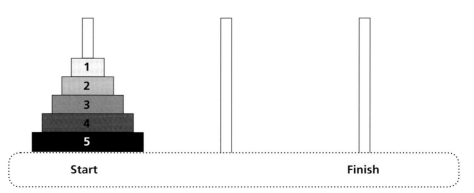

Towers of Hanoi

Incident 2 – Brainteaser

Set the Patrol a riddle or lateral thinking problem, such as the one below and give them 10 minutes to solve it.

Situation: You are in a prison. There are four prisoners who have been given an assignment; they are placed as follows:

Number one is placed behind the prison wall and is looking in the opposite direction, away from the wall. Number two is placed on the other side of the wall and is looking right at the wall. Number three is behind Number two and Number four is behind Number three. They are all looking in the same direction.

The prisoners are each wearing a hat and they have been told that two of the hats are black and the other two are white. Their assignment is to figure out which colour hat they are wearing. They are allowed one guess each. Whoever guesses correctly will get their freedom.

You are now told that the line up is black, white, black, white (as below) but the prisoners aren't told. Who will guess it and why?

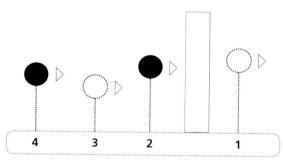

The four prisoners

Solution: It can't be Number one, due to the fact that he can not see any of the others.

Number two has the same problem. Number four has the best chance because he can see two of the others. If he saw that the two in front of him were wearing the same colour hat, he would be sure that his hat was the opposite colour. Due to the fact that this is not the case, he has to reconsider his guess.

Number three is thinking that, as Number four hasn't tried to use his guess, then it is obvious that he and Number two are wearing different colour hats. He will guess the opposite colour to Number two, i.e. white!

Incident 3 – Needle in a haystack

A simple hide and seek exercise. You hide a small object (e.g. a key) in a marked out area before the team arrive. They have ten minutes to find it. No clues, no riddles, just a thorough examination of the area is required. Be inventive and hide the item in bowls of custard, jelly, up a tree, in a hole and so on.

Incident 4 – Balloon burst

Set up a three-tiered target area on grass with bamboo canes. On this area, blow up and distribute balloons of various shapes and sizes. Explain that the task is to pop as many balloons as possible in the ten minutes using a bow and arrow. You may need a couple of minutes to demonstrate correct use of the arrow. Explain that balloons in the top row count for three points, the middle ones are two points and the bottom row is one point.

Ideally use a sloped area of grass. Patrol members should take it in turns to fire a small number of arrows in one turn.

Incident 5 – Backwoods cooking

Make chocolate bananas. Check dietary requirements first and provide alternatives if there are any Scouts who cannot eat chocolate or bananas. Cut the banana open lengthways, fill with flaky chocolate pieces, close up, wrap up in foil and place in the embers of a lit fire. Leave for eight minutes. Eat and enjoy.

Incident 6 – Stretcher assault course

Give the Patrol a canvas bag (such as a tent bag, two 2m poles and some rope). Tell them they have ten minutes to make a stretcher that will carry the smallest member of the Patrol around an obstacle course and complete the course as a team.

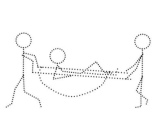

GAMES NIGHTS

There are occasions when the Scouts will like nothing more than an evening packed full of games. This is not necessarily an evening of football, although once in a while it could be. A games night can offer the opportunity to try a wide variety of games, including individual challenges, team sports, relay races and games that the whole Troop can play together.

Meetings like this are especially welcome when the day has been wet and the school have not allowed their students out at break time. Equally, during exam time, many Scouts will enjoy the opportunity to just 'let off steam.' It is important to vary the choice of games, as Scouts will tire of any activity that becomes too familiar.

Everybody in!

These are games in which members of the Troop play as individuals against the rest of the Troop.

Knockout games

These are games where the objective is for the individual player, team or Patrol, to try to knock their opponent out of the game. The winner is the last remaining player, team or Patrol.

Pairs games

These games are for the whole Troop and involve one pair of players competing against each other at a time.

Two-team games

These are games in which the Troop divides into two competing teams.

Patrol competitions

These are games where three or more small teams compete together. Such games can help a Patrol develop by encouraging its members to interact, to support one another, to tolerate each other's weaknesses and to appreciate strengths. For the Patrol Leader, or older Scouts, there is the opportunity to practice leadership skills and develop a 'game plan.'

Interactive games

These are games where one member of a Patrol or team competes against representatives from each of the other teams.

Races and relays

Unlike most other team games, races and relays are not interactive and do not tend to involve teamwork or tactics. However, they do enable players to demonstrate people skills. Leaders can therefore use the games to test a player either before or after training.

Sports games

These games are variations of popular sports, such as football, cricket and rounders.

Run-scoring games

The aim of this type of game is to score points by running between two bases, lines or wickets. The number of runs will depend on the skill with which the object, usually a ball, is hit, kicked or thrown.

Wide games

A wide game is a game played over a wide area, such as a park, field, campsite or in a wooded area. It should be a secure area with easily defined boundaries to prevent players wandering off and getting lost. Most wide games last about 45 to 90 minutes, so they can be run on a Troop night as well as during a camp. They can be played in daylight, or in the dark. Wide games fall into four basic types, although some are a combination of two or more:

1. Cordon-breaking: Getting through a guarded cordon, usually to deliver a message

2. Manhunt: Locating a person or persons

3. Treasure hunt: Finding clues and treasure

4. Raid: Raiding an opponent's base, while defending your own

Training games

These are games or exercises that can be used to teach or test specific Scout skills. Many of the other games listed above can also be adapted for this purpose.

THEME NIGHTS

Some Troop nights can be built around a single theme. This allows a range of activities to be explored in one Programme Zone or one specific part of a Programme Zone.

Survival Night

For example, a survival meeting night might include some or all of the following activities:

- Building a shelter
- Building bivouacs
- Using survival bags
- Making survival kits
- Emergency foods
- Developing the senses of taste, smell, touch, hearing and sight
- Tracking and following trails
- Lighting fires
- Cooking survival meals
- Plant recognition
- Emergency signalling.

A programme based around the theme of 'East and West' might look like this:

Meeting programme for 10 June

Time	Activity
7.00	Opening
7.15	Port/Starboard (using North, South, East, West)
7.30	3 x 20 minute bases
8.30	Taste test
9.00	Closing – reflection using paper cranes

East and West – 20 minute bases

Group A	Group B	Group C
Origami	Corn cobs	Bucking bronco
BBQ meat	Bucking bronco	Origami
Bucking bronco	Origami	Chinese stir-fry

Origami – Paper-folding exercise to make a paper crane; a symbol of hope in Japan. Instructions from Programmes Online (www.scouts.org.uk/pol).

Cooking – Each group prepares a different part of the meal for the taste test at the end of the meeting. Corn cobs are prepared by cutting in half and skewering with forks. These are dipped in butter and turned on the BBQ grill for 10 minutes. Explain that this is a traditional food of the Wild West, in parts of America such as Mexico. BBQ is a flavour associated with the West (as well as being popular as part of a modern British summertime!) Get one group to coat and grill different meats (and vegetable kebabs if you have vegetarians). For an eastern dish, stirfry some vegetables, adding a sauce such as sweet chilli, soy or black bean. Serve all the dishes buffet-style for the taste test.

Remember to check food allergies/dietary requirements prior to activity.

Bucking bronco – visit from Stu (local fairground manager) with rodeo machine. Set up in main hall, with each group having 20 minutes to have a go. Keep on during taste test if possible and run competition with each group's nominee.

Kit needed

Origami – Square pieces of paper, one each plus some spare

Cooking – BBQ grills, forks, paper plates/cutlery, utensils, wok, kitchen area, ingredients as required.

Bucking bronco - rodeo equipment brought by Stu, space needed in hall.

Run by

Origami – Sue

Cooking – Hugh

Bucking Bronco - Stu

VISITS

Troop nights do not always need to revolve around the Troop Meeting Place and certainly during the summer months, Scouts should be out and about. With a little organisation, the meeting can be held at one of many venues. The most obvious are fire or police stations, but there are a number of facilities that can be visited for a Troop meeting by all or part of the Troop. Some examples include:

- ten-pin bowling alley
- swimming pool
- sports stadium
- local park or country park
- campsite or activity centre
- newspaper offices or printers
- Scout Gang show

- sewage works
- farm
- telephone exchange
- hospital
- ambulance station
- lifeboat station
- factory
- 24-hr shop or service station
- places of worship
- bell tower.

Different destinations for your visits offer a variety of further activity opportunities. For example, a visit to a local sports complex can link into the Fitness Challenge or one of the Activity Badges. A visit to a sewage works could provide a way into environmental issues.

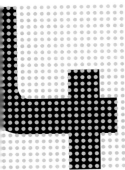

4 GENERATING IDEAS

A RESOURCE LIKE THIS CAN ONLY INCLUDE A LIMITED NUMBER OF IDEAS. TROOPS OPERATE IN A WIDE VARIETY OF ENVIRONMENTS AND CONDITIONS SO MUCH OF THE PROGRAMME MUST DEPEND ON THE IMAGINATION OF THE LEADERSHIP TEAM. HERE ARE SOME EFFECTIVE WAYS OF GENERATING NEW IDEAS FOR PROGRAMMES.

BRAINSTORMING

Brainstorming is a technique used to get a lot of ideas from a group in a short space of time. The emphasis is on the number of ideas and you must accept that much of what can be suggested may never be used. The more people involved, the more ideas generated, so consider using all your leadership team as well as some of your Scouts, local Explorer Scouts and even parents or carers.

Everyone is encouraged to put forward an idea in turn, no matter how wild or silly it may appear. This can produce lots of noise and laughter, which is useful, as many people are able to be more creative when in a relaxed and humorous environment. All the ideas should be recorded and in the early stages no one should comment or disregard any of the ideas. Indeed, a seemingly foolish idea from one person may just spark off a brilliant idea from someone else. Have plenty of large sheets of paper fixed to the wall, a supply of pens and a 'scribe' to note everything down.

The second stage

Having created your list, the second stage is to look at those which people think are practical, possible or just fun to try. If the ideas are for a large-scale project, you may ask two or three people to take the idea away and develop it further. The ideas you choose can then become part of the programme.

Brainstorming can be more focused by taking a particular theme as the starting point. For example, any one of the Programme Zones could start you off. You could even use the letters of the alphabet and chart ideas for each letter, as follows:

A Abseiling, Aids awareness, aviation

B Backwoods cooking, bike rides, Belfast (HMS)

C Camping, canoeing, circus skills

D Dennis fire engines, diving, darts

BUZZ GROUPS

Buzz groups are useful for making sure that everyone can contribute their ideas. Sometimes Scouts are shy about sharing ideas. Talking about their ideas with one or two others before feeding these into a larger group or writing individual's ideas on a Post-it Note can help make sure that even the quietest members of the Troop can put forward suggestions.

Generating Ideas
:> Brainstorming
:> Buzz Groups
:> Mind Mapping
Idea Boxes
Other Sources of Ideas

MIND-MAPPING

Mind-maps, or spider grams as they are sometimes called, are done in a similar way to brainstorming. Only this time a focus word or subject is placed in the centre of the sheet. You might want to pick a theme and see how many linking ideas you can generate. You could put one of the Programme Zones in the centre of your sheet and explore how many activities you can chart.

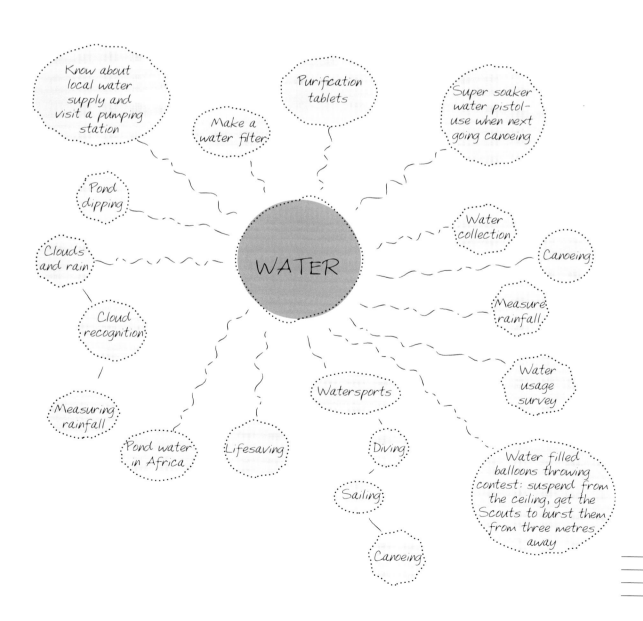

IDEA BOXES

Another way of generating programme ideas is to divide a large sheet of paper into 16 squares, each with a heading of an activity area. The Scouts then have the opportunity to write in suggestions for an appropriate activity in each box. This is an excellent way of involving Scouts in the planning of meetings. You can either provide every Scout with a marker pen, or, better still, give each Scout a pen and a few Post-it Notes.

Scoutcraft skills	Away from the Troop room	Adventurous activities	International activities
Lightweight pioneering Building shelters	Chip survey All day city wide game	Racing Helm Badge Dinghy Sailor Badge Scout Canoeist	Host to visiting Scouts from Germany Email links to Scouts overseas
Outdoor activities	**Team building**	**Cooking activities**	**Community activities**
Cycle-skills event Skateboard challenge Beach games	Older Scout Winter camp Incident hike	Sweet making Cooking vegetarian at camp Hay box cooking	Glass recycling project Sponsored World food day
Health and fitness	**Away from the Troop**	**Community activities**	**Adventurous activities**
Football contest Beach games competition	Day visit to London Visit to Lego Land	Bag packing in supermarket Visit to Temple	40km canoe paddle Winter hill walking experience (with County Team)
Joint activities	**Camping activities**	**Invited guests**	**Scoutcraft skills**
Joint camp with the 19th Older Cub Scout/younger Scout activity day	36 hour 'survival camp' 'Winter 'indoor' camp	The 'Owl Man' Local Beat Officer	Raft building Commando Bridge Pioneering Badge

OTHER SOURCES OF IDEAS

Other sources for helping to generate good programme ideas include:

- Directories, such as Yellow Pages and Thomson's

- Local guidebooks

- Old Moore's Almanac

- Dates and festivals, such as Patron Saints' days, religious festivals, anniversaries.

5 BADGES AND AWARDS

SCOUTS LIKE TO EARN BADGES. OVER THE YEARS, BADGES HAVE BEEN USED BOTH TO ENCOURAGE YOUNG PEOPLE TO TRY SOMETHING NEW AND ALSO TO RECOGNISE ACHIEVEMENTS AND ABILITY DEMONSTRATED ELSEWHERE.

The Programme includes many opportunities for young people to gain badges:

 • Membership Award

 • Participation Awards

 • Challenge Badges

 • Activity Badges

 • Partnership Awards

MEMBERSHIP AWARD

This award helps Scouts understand the commitment they are making when they make their Promise and become Members of the worldwide family of Scouting and of the Scout section.

The requirements

When a young person joins the Troop, regardless of whether he or she was a Cub Scout, the following requirements will need to be completed to gain this award:

- Get to know the other members and leaders in the Patrol and Troop

- Know what to do at the investiture

- Find out about the ceremonies and traditions in the Troop

- Find out about the activities that the Patrol and Troop does

- Know and understand the Scout Promise and Law and the rules of the Troop

- Know and understand the Scout Motto, Sign, Salute and Handshake

- Show a general knowledge of the history and family of Scouts and Scouting around the world

PARTICIPATION AWARDS

In the Troop, up to five Participation Awards can be earned. They would normally be presented one-year after the Scout has joined the Troop. Alternatively, if the young person has been a member of the Cub Scout Pack, this will happen a year after the badge was presented. The award celebrates a young person's commitment to Scouting and their active involvement in a Balanced Programme. The presentation will be an opportunity to remind the Scout what they have achieved in the last twelve months. It is also a chance to look forward to all the opportunities leading up to the presentation of the next award, the following year. Some Troops award a Participation badge around the time of a Scout's birthday.

ADAPTING BADGES AND AWARDS

The requirements for badges and awards provide a wide range of choice for all Scouts. Most Scouts will be able to access the badges and awards of their choice. There will be a number of children with special needs who will need further flexibility to gain badges and awards. Adaptation may be required specifically to the needs of the child concerned. The aim in each case should be to improve access to the badges and awards rather than to reduce the challenge of the requirements. In other words it should still be a challenge, but an achievable one.

→ ROUTE TO THE CHIEF SCOUT'S GOLD AWARD

The Chief Scout's Gold Award is the highest award a Scout can gain in the Scout Section. The route to the Chief Scout's Award is by completing Challenges from different areas of the programme. Many of the activities they undertake as a Scout will count towards their Challenges and therefore also towards this prestigious Award. While you will probably keep central records of your Scout's achievements, they should be encouraged to keep a record of what they achieve in their own copy of *The Scout Record Book*. They will need to get eight Challenges to gain the Chief Scout's Gold Award.

Please note: Outdoor Plus, Adventure and Expedition Challenges provide extended choice in the Outdoor Zone of the Balanced Programme.

To gain your Chief Scout's Gold Award earn each of these Challenge Awards:

Plus two of these awards:

Chief Scout's Gold Award	Promise	Community	Fitness	Creative	Global	Outdoor	Outdoor Plus	Adventure	Expedition

→ CHALLENGE BADGES

→ COMMUNITY CHALLENGE

Complete the activities in the two following areas. Examples are provided below but other activities can also be undertaken.

Area 1 – Exploring the local community

Explore one aspect of how the local community works and is organised to the benefit of its members. The project should include some fact-finding, a visit to or from a community facility or group and some form of report back.

For example: visits to see the workings of a theatre, tourist attraction, railway station, airport, local industry; chances to meet people involved in local government, charities, faith groups, interest groups; opportunities to hear about/take part in community traditions/customs, local clubs and interest groups.

Area 2 – Community service

Take an active part in some form of local community service totalling at least six hours. The time may be spent doing a number of different projects or by showing commitment to a single project over a longer period of time.

For example: running a fund-raising stall or game; delivering leaflets, clearing an area, gardening, collecting materials for recycling, helping with activities for younger children; moving furniture, clearing debris, painting fences, environmental projects. Where possible the service should link in with the visit in Area 1.

→ **FITNESS CHALLENGE**

Complete the activities from one of the following two areas, demonstrating a noticeable improvement in the chosen discipline:

Area 1 - Physical Challenge

Choose a physical challenge which is new or which builds on an earlier achievement.

The challenge could be an athletic event, a charity swim, a long distance cycle ride, a pool life-saving test or a long distance challenge hike. Indeed, it could be any event that requires the need to physically train in order to succeed. Consider a variety of activities/interests in choosing this challenge, and agree your choice with a Leader.

To complete the challenge:

a. Spend between four and six weeks preparing for the event, through an agreed programme of activity/training.

b. Show an understanding of the importance of a sensible and appropriate diet and the need for sufficient sleep.

c. Be able to explain the dangers and harmful effects of smoking, alcohol and drugs.

d. Successfully take part in the chosen physical challenge.

Area 2 - Physical Development

Choose a physical activity, which you wish to develop.

For example: circuit training, football skill training, aerobics routine, light weight training.

To complete the challenge:

a. Exercise regularly over a period of four to six weeks and keep a record that shows improvement over this period.

b. Show an understanding of the importance of a sensible and appropriate diet, and the need for sufficient sleep.

c. Be able to explain the dangers and harmful effects of smoking, alcohol and drugs.

→ **CREATIVE CHALLENGE**

Complete activities from three of the following six areas:

Area 1 – Performing

Take part in a performance in front of an audience.

For example: short play, series of sketches, performing magic tricks, singing, playing a musical instrument, a Scout Show, a dance, or a puppet show.

Area 2 – Crafts

Have a go at some creative crafts.

For example: glass painting, macramé, art-straws, leatherwork, photography, sweet making, decorative knotting, or candle making.

Area 3 – Promotions

Promote local Scouting.

For example: a newsletter, poster, video, website, audio-based broadcast, or display.

Area 4 – Problem solving

Take an active part in activities requiring a number of problem-solving skills, effective teamwork and creative thinking.

For example: Incident hikes or timed challenges, mental, physical or skill.

Area 5 - Construction

Construct a model.

For example: model aircraft, 3-D jigsaw, model pioneering project, or model campsite.

Area 6 – Worship

Take a leading role in preparing and participating in an Act of Worship or Scouts' Own.

For example: selecting or writing, prayers or music. This could be at a Troop meeting, residential experience or event.

→ **GLOBAL CHALLENGE**

Complete all the activities in one of the following two areas:

Area 1: International contact

Make contact with Scouts from another country outside the United Kingdom.

Then

Take part in a Troop or Patrol activity with these Scouts.

or

Take part in a Patrol or Troop activity based on things found out during the International contact.

This can be done a number of ways, for example through Nights Away in the UK or overseas, the Internet, pen pals, Jamboree-on-the-Air (JOTA), Jamboree-on-the-Internet (JOTI), or Lands of Adventure.

Area 2: International issues

Choose and investigate an international issue. For example:

a. Trade

b. Health

c. Water & sanitation

d. Environment

e. Conflict

f. Refugees

g. Peace

h. Tourism

i. Homelessness

j. Poverty

k. Animal welfare

l. Conservation.

Then complete the following:

a. Show an understanding of the issues involved.

b. Take some action as a result of research

c. Compare how the issues affect the UK and countries overseas.

→ **PROMISE CHALLENGE**

Complete five activities in total, taken from at least two areas. Examples are provided below but other similar activities can also be undertaken.

Area 1 - Commitment to the Promise and Scout Law

a. Explain how you have recently 'done your best' on at least three occasions and how this has made a difference.

b. Explain to a new Scout in your Troop the meaning of the Scout Promise and Law.

c. Assist with the planning and take part in an investiture ceremony or similar.

d. Demonstrate that you can be trusted by taking on a special responsibility on behalf of the Troop. This might involve the management of money, or the Troop's reputation.

Area 2 - Relationship with your God

a. Take part in a number of acts of worship with others in the Troop, such as Scout Parades at your place of worship, and/or Scouts' Owns.

b. Complete a course that furthers your understanding of your own faith community.

c. Choose and read prayers and/or reflections for your Troop's opening and closing ceremony.

d. Hold the My Faith Activity Badge.

Area 3 - The life of the Troop

a. Take an active part in at least two Troop Forums and express your views on at least one item being discussed.

b. Contribute to the writing or reviewing of your Troop's 'Code of Conduct.'

c. Play a full part in at least two Troop Leadership Forums and help to implement a decision of the forum.

d. Successfully run a learning experience for other Scouts.

e. Successfully lead a group of Scouts at a two-day camp or other similar event.

Area 4 - Developing beliefs and attitudes

a. Honestly review an event or activity and decide how it might be done better in the future.

b. Visit an act of worship of another faith community and compare the traditions and customs with your own.

c. Investigate a political or world issue, such as climate change, smoking, fair trade and explain your views to others on the subject.

d. Take part in a debate on a topic of local or national interest.

e. As a Scout, give freely of your time to help someone less fortunate than yourself.

→ **OUTDOOR CHALLENGE**

Take an active part in one or more Nights Away, totalling at least two nights, preferably camping, to include many of the following activities:

a. Help to pitch and strike your tent.

b. Light a fire and cook at least one meal using an open fire.

c. Set up a suitable stove, and prepare a meal using a stove.

d. Demonstrate personal hygiene.

e. Keep your belongings organised and tidy within your accommodation.

f. Maintain a tidy and orderly site.

g. Take part in a wide game.

h. Take part in a campfire or other entertainment.

i. Build a simple pioneering project.

j. Build a useful camp gadget.

k. Explore the environment of your camp.

l. With others, successfully complete a two hour activity or project.

m. Provide a service commitment to the site for about an hour.

This list gives an idea of the type and style of the activities that the Nights Away should include. Depending on the activity there may be extra ideas that could be included, which can be agreed in the Troop Forum.

In addition to the above, demonstrate the following basic emergency aid skills during the Nights Away experience:

a. Understand the initial actions to take in the event of an accident.

b. Understand the importance of getting adult help and when to call the emergency services.

c. Know how to treat minor cuts, burns and scalds, stings and insect bites.

→ **OUTDOOR PLUS CHALLENGE**

Complete the following activities:

• Hold the Outdoor Challenge.

• Have spent at least eight nights away as a Scout, four of which must be camping.

• Take an active part in further camp(s), which should include many of the following:

a. Lead or help to lead a group of Scouts in setting up a well-organised site that includes sleeping tents, food and equipment stores, fire/stove, kitchen and eating area.

b. Plan a balanced menu for a short camp.

c. Show how to use safely an axe and/or a saw.

d. Lead the cooking of a meal for the group.

e. Show knowledge of the safety precautions for the use of lamps and stoves.

f. Cook a backwoods meal with the group.

g. Build a working camp gadget, such as an altar fire, camp oven or a gateway to a campsite.

h. Take a leading role in the construction of a pioneering project.

i. Build a bivouac and sleep in it.

Note: This list gives an idea of the type and style of the activities that the Nights Away should include. Depending on the activity there may be extra ideas that could be included, which can be agreed in the Troop Forum.

• In addition to the above, demonstrate knowledge in emergency aid for the outdoors and be able to:

a. Demonstrate how to open an airway and give CPR.

b. Know how and when to put a patient in the recovery position.

c. Know how to recognise and treat fractures and severe bleeding.

d. Know how to use direct pressure to stop bleeding.

e. Demonstrate an awareness of the dangers of temperature extremes such as sunstroke, dehydration, heat exhaustion and hypothermia and know how to prevent and treat them.

→ **ADVENTURE CHALLENGE**

Take part in three different activities, ideally on separate occasions. Examples of various suitable activities are given below. This is a guideline rather than a complete list.

Adventure activities

- Climbing
- Hill walking
- Hiking
- Explore a town or area you don't know.
- Orienteering
- Plan and undertake a journey by public transport.
- Caving or pot holing
- Pony trekking or horse riding
- Cycling
- Sailing
- Canoeing
- Water-skiing
- Surfing
- Dragon boating
- Bellboating
- Sub-aqua

- Canal boating
- Rafting
- Pulling
- Gliding
- Powered aircraft
- Hovercrafting
- Stunt kiting
- Hot air ballooning
- Paragliding

For each activity:

Know the safety issues involved and understand the use of any equipment needed for the activity.

Show an awareness of environmental issues around the activity (such as erosion at popular climbing areas).

Know about further opportunities to take part in the chosen activities.

→ **EXPEDITION CHALLENGE**

Complete the activities in one of the following two areas:

Area 1 - Expedition – 'A journey with a purpose'

Take part in an expedition over two days (including a night away) with at least three friends. Be involved in the planning of the expedition, complete relevant training and be properly prepared.

During the expedition:

a. Play a full part in the team.
b. Journey for at least four hours each day.
c. Use a map to keep track of where you are.
d. Stay overnight at a hostel or other suitable venue, or camp overnight at a suitable site.
e. Cook the evening meal and breakfast.
f. Achieve at least one goal, agreed with your Leader before the expedition.

The expedition may be on foot, canoe, cycle or sailing boat. Other options may be appropriate, and should be agreed beforehand.

Notes: Scouts must be supervised taking into account their preparation, training and level of experience. This may mean that certain legs are 'led' by young people themselves for information/ project purposes. As a minimum, supervision involves a visual check on departure and at the end of each day, and being in the area of the activity. The Scout Association Permit Scheme applies to certain land terrains and classifications of water. You can check the individual requirements of an activity by visiting the A to Z of Activities on www.scouts.org.uk. To lead a night's away experience, a young person is required to hold a Nights Away Event Passport.

Area 2 - Exploration – 'A purpose with a journey'

Take part in an exploration over two days (including a night away) with at least three friends, and report or present your findings. You must be involved in the planning of the exploration, complete relevant training and be properly prepared. You must have completed some initial research into the subject to be investigated. The challenge should take place somewhere you have never been before or don't know well.

During the exploration:

a. Play a full part in the team.
b. Travel for at least 90 minutes to a hostel, campsite or other suitable venue.
c. Use a map to keep track of where you are.
d. Conduct the exploration within an agreed area (discussed with a Leader in advance. collecting evidence and information for the report or presentation.
e. Stay overnight at the venue and cook the evening meal and breakfast.
f. Complete the exploration before returning home.
g. Have the report or presentation ready within four weeks of the exploration.

The journey may be on foot, or by public transport, canoe, cycle, aircraft, wheelchair or boat. Other options may be possible and should be agreed beforehand.

Note: The 'exploration' element should last 4-5 hours over the two days. It could be anything from an investigation into bird life in a wood to visiting museums in a town.

→ ACTIVITY BADGES

NOTE

For activity badges that require Scouts to 'gain' or 'qualify for' an external award, it is only necessary to meet the requirements for such awards, and there is no obligation to attend an external course if the syllabus can be covered by the instructor

→ ADMINISTRATOR

Complete the requirements below:

1. Choose one of these activities:

a. Type 200 words using a word processor or desktop publisher, ensuring that there are no mistakes before printing it out.

b. Write 100 words of prose in a good legible hand.

2. Show a good general knowledge of the administrative arrangements in a Scout Group. This should include the key roles and responsibilities of the Group Scout Leader, or of the Chairman, Secretary and Treasurer of the Group Executive Committee.

3. Know how a personal bank account operates.

4. After consultation with a member of the leadership team, draft a letter on an agreed subject and share this with this person.

5. Draft an invitation card for members of the public in connection with a Group, Troop or Patrol event. Share this with a member of the leadership team.

6. Choose one of these activities:

a. Prepare a press release on a Group, Troop or Patrol event.

b. Write an article for a magazine/newsletter reporting on a Group, Troop or Patrol event.

7. Carry out the duties of secretary of a committee (this could be a Troop Forum, school club or council etc). These should include taking of minutes/action points, duplication and circulation.

→ AERONAUTICS

Complete all the requirements in one of the following alternatives:

Alternative A

1. Know the rules relating to access to airfields in *Policy, Organisation and Rules*.

2. Understand the purpose and operation of ailerons, rudder, elevator and trim on a glider and have the effects of these controls demonstrated in flight.

3. Understand the functions and workings of the altimeter, airspeed indicator and variometer.

4. Assist a glider pilot with the ground handling, hangar parking and launching of his aircraft.

5. Demonstrate the signals used by the glider pilot and forward signaller for the launching of a glider and the procedure for stopping a launch.

Alternative B

1. Know the rules relating to access to airfields in *Policy, Organisation and Rules*.

2. Assist a pilot with ground handling, the picketing of a light aircraft and the preparation of a light aircraft for flight.

3. Understand the purpose and operation of ailerons, rudder elevator, flaps and trim on a light aircraft and have the effects of these controls demonstrated in flight.

4. Understand the functions and workings of the altimeter, airspeed indicator and engine instrumentation.

5. Demonstrate the marshalling signals used when marshalling powered aircraft. Identify the common signals displayed on the airfield signal square.

6. Understand the R/T procedure for a circuit of an airfield.

Alternative C

1. Know the rules relating to access to airfields in *Policy, Organisation and Rules*.

2. Demonstrate the marshalling signals used when marshalling powered aircraft;

Badges and Awards

Participation Awards

Chief Scout's Gold Award

Challenge Badges

Activity Badges

Administrator

Aeronautics

Air Researcher

Air Spotter

Staged Activity Badges

Activity Plus Badges

Instructor Badges

Partnership Awards

or demonstrate the signals used by a glider pilot and forward signaller for the launching of a glider and the procedure for stopping a launch.

3. Identify the parts of an aircraft and explain their functions in controlling the aircraft.

4. Assist with the ground handling and picketing of a light aircraft or the ground handling, rigging and de-rigging of a glider.

5. Demonstrate the ground checks that have to be carried out before flying a light aircraft or glider.

6. Demonstrate an ability to carry out two of the following:

a. Tie knots and make splices used in glider launching equipment.

b. Repair a small tear in the fabric surface of a light aircraft or glider.

c. Replenish a light aircraft's fuel system.

d. Carry out pre-use inspection of a parachute. Demonstrate how to put it on and take it off.

e. Assist with the launching of a hot air balloon.

f. Know the procedure for starting up a piston-engined aircraft.

→ **AIR RESEARCHER**

Complete the requirements below:

1. Know the safety rules with regard to access to airfields in *Policy, Organisation and Rules*.

2. Carry out research into one historical aspect of flight, and share your findings with others in the Troop. Example research topics include the following:

a. The development of aviation or flight over a period agreed with your assessor.

b. The development of a specific aircraft type, discovering details of its history, role and achievements. Examples include: Spitfire, Boeing 747, Harrier or Wessex helicopter.

c. The development of balloons or airships from their first appearance to the present day.

d. The development of a type of aero engine. Examples might be jet or piston engines in general, or a specific engine such as the Rolls Royce Merlin.

3. In the course of your research, visit at least one place of interest that is directly relevant to your project. For example a museum, an air display or an aeronautics factory.

4. The presentation of your findings should include a model that you have made to illustrate some aspect of your research. Other resource materials such as diagrams and pictures should be used wherever possible.

→ **AIR SPOTTER**

Complete the requirements below:

1. Be able to recognise by sight, three-quarters of the aircraft in the list published by The Scout Association. (The Scout Information Centre has a free Aircraft Recognition CD for this purpose).

2. Complete one of the following activities:

a. By yourself or with another Scout, take photographs or collect pictures of a minimum of ten different aircraft types found in Europe. Name the different types and their uses.

b. Keep a log for at least four weeks including dates and times. Note the aircraft seen (giving any distinctive recognition features) and the aircraft's approximate heading.

3. Complete one of the following activities:

a. Recognise and name national aircraft markings, both service and civil, of at least six countries including the United Kingdom.

b. Understand the RAF and NATO system of letter designation according to aircraft function and give examples of three such designations.

c. Name three basic training aircraft used in private flying. Give a brief report on one, naming a club and airfield where it is used (local, wherever possible).

4. Describe the key recognition features of six aircraft selected by an appropriate adult.

→ ANGLER

Complete the requirements below:

Health and safety

1. Know the water safety rules and the appropriate precautions to be taken when fishing from the bank or shore, or from a boat. Understand the dangers of wading in fresh water and shore fishing in the sea and the precautions to be taken.

2. Know the basic hygiene precautions to take when fishing.

Angling craft

3. Go fishing in fresh or salt water on at least six occasions, recording the following:

   • numbers caught

   • species and size of fish

   • method, tackle and bait used

   • weather and water conditions

Discuss the trips undertaken.

4. Explain the signs of stress in fish. Know the Environment Agency Emergency Hotline number.

Tackle and techniques

5. Understand why it is important to discard used tackle properly.

6. Choose one of the following activities:

a. Cast with beach fishing tackle a distance of 45 metres.

b. Cast a ledger and float tackle into a 1-metre circle at least three times out of six at nine metres range.

c. Cast a trout fly on a fly line into a 3-metre circle at least three times out of eight at 11-metre range.

7. Demonstrate how to set up one of the following sets of tackle:

   • waggler rig

   • swim feeder rig

   • fly cast

   • spinning rig

   • shore fishing rig

   • beach casting rig

8. Explain the importance of:

a. handling fish with care and releasing them carefully

b. using a lower strength hook link when coarse, game or sea fishing.

9. Explain the importance of the one of the following activities:

a. Setting a keep net correctly

b. How to use a priest to despatch fish quickly.

Know your fish

10. Be able to identify each of the species in one of the following groups:

a. Bass, cod, flounder, grey mullet, and mackerel

b. Roach, perch, chub, common carp and tench

c. Grayling, brown trout, rainbow trout and salmon.

11. Know the habitat and feeding behaviour of the fish identified and know suitable baits, flies, lures and hook sizes.

Administration and law

Complete the requirements from either of the options below:

12. Freshwater fishing

a. Know the dates of the fresh water season and size limits of freshwater fish in the areas in which you fish.

b. Be able to explain why licenses and permits are required for fishing and know the age at which a national rod licence is required.

c. Know the location of the local fishing club and any waters they may control.

13. Saltwater fishing

a. Know the size limits of saltwater fish in the areas in which you fish.

b. Be able to explain why licences and permits are required for fishing and know the age at which a national rod licence is required.

→ ARTIST

Complete the requirements below:

1. Paint or draw an illustration of a scene from a story agreed beforehand.

2. Paint or draw either a person from life or an object set before you.

3. Paint or draw a landscape as agreed with an appropriate adult.

4. Show a selection of your recent work.

Note: A computer drawing package may be used.

→ ARTS ENTHUSIAST

Complete the requirements below:

1. Take an active interest in a particular art form or artist. For example, this could be painting, pop music, sculpture, theatre, architecture, break dancing or similar. The interest could also be in a favourite artist.

2. Describe two visits made in relation to the interest. They might include photographs, film, recordings, concert programmes, ticket stubs, newspaper reviews, websites or other aids.

3. Demonstrate a detailed knowledge of a particular aspect of the interest. For instance, a particular painting, performance, sculpture, building or similar; or a particular person, movement or period connected with the chosen art form.

4. List major events, exhibitions or venues connected with the chosen art form or artist and be able to discuss their significance.

Note: The particular art form or artist to be chosen should be discussed with an appropriate adult beforehand.

→ ASTRONAUTICS

Complete the requirements below:

1. Explain the purpose of space exploration including:

- Historical reasons

- Immediate goals in terms of specific knowledge

- Benefits related to Earth resources, technology, and new products.

2. Chose one topic below and with it undertake Option One or Two:

a. A commercial or scientific rocket (Ariane, Delta, Soyuz, Proton, Zenit, etc).

b. The NASA Space Shuttle

c. The International Space Station

d. A specific satellite (e.g. Envisat, Cassini, Aurora, etc).

e. An unmanned space probe.

Option one

Describe the topic's primary mission purpose; explain the functions of the component parts, together with a brief history and accomplishments of a specific mission and what was learned from that mission.

Option two

Build a scale model of or about the topic, either from a commercial kit, or from plans available from the Internet or model clubs and shops.

3. Discuss and demonstrate two of the following:

a. The law of action-reaction in the context of rockets and zero or low-gravity environments.

b. How rocket engines work, and their lift-off and re-entry procedures.

c. How satellites stay in orbit and the different types of orbits they use

d. How satellite pictures of the Earth, planets and their moons are made and transmitted.

4. Complete all of the activities in one of the following alternatives:

Alternative A – Rocketry

1. Explain the Safety Code for Rocketry and be able to identify the principal parts of a rocket.

2. Describe how solid and liquid propellant rocket motors work.

3. Build, launch, and recover a single or double-staged model rocket.

4. Make a second launch to accomplish a specific objective. For example, carrying a fragile payload, aerial photography, altitude measurement, temperature measurement, parachute recovery, remote control, building a launch controller or launch pad.

Note: This activity must follow the appropriate BMFA/UKRA safety codes on rocketry.

Alternative B - Space Exploration

1. Describe how space satellites and probes have added to our knowledge of the Solar System.

2. Build an accurate scale model of a space exploration vehicle. Find out about its design, function, and basic operation. Be able to help others learn about your vehicle.

3. Design an inhabited base space colony. What conditions will you need to overcome to ensure suitable living arrangements, energy sources, special equipment, health and safety needs, and environmental protection or danger? Share and explain your design or model with others.

4. Using photographs, news clippings, electronic/internet articles etc, mount a display about a current space mission and share your findings with others.

Alternative C - Space Port

1. With a group of Scouts, plan and participate in a themed 'Space Camp' or event, undertaking appropriate activities.

2. Assist in organising a visit to a space centre, museum, planetarium or rocketry enthusiasts group and share your experiences with an adult or other Scouts.

3. Find out about careers in the space industry.

→ **ASTRONOMER**

Complete the requirements below:

1. Demonstrate an understanding of the night sky and why the pattern of stars changes night by night throughout the year. Know the meaning of the terms celestial equator and poles; circumpolar; and zodiac.

2. Recognise the main constellations and know the names of some of their important stars.

3. Know the meaning of four of the astronomical terms below and where to find examples of:

a. An open star cluster (Pleiades, Hyades, Praesepe, Double Cluster in Perseus)

b. A globular cluster (Hercules)

c. A double star (Mizar and Alcor, Albireo, Epsilon Lyrae)

d. Another galaxy (Andromeda)

e. A nebula (Orion)

f. A red giant (Betelgeuse).

4. Give a general description of the Sun, individual planets, moons, comets and meteor showers, asteroids and meteorites. Know that the Solar System is part of the Milky Way galaxy.

5. Know about man's activities in space, to include SOHO, Hubble, Cassini, and the International Space Station.

6. Explain how the Moon affects the tides. Be able to advise on the state of the tide by using a tide table.

7. Visit a planetarium, observatory or science centre; or explore an aspect of astronomy further using relevant Internet sites.

8. Undertake a project of your choice for three months to further your understanding of astronomy before meeting again with your assessor to discuss your project. Example projects include the following:

a. Keep a diary of planetary events.

b. Record meteor showers and satellites seen while observing the night sky.

c. Keep a log of Moon halos and phases of the Moon.

d. Collect newspaper or magazine cuttings or website pages reporting on space missions across the world.

e. Maintain a general interest in astronomy and then meet again with your assessor to discuss your experience.

→ ATHLETICS

Complete the requirements below:

1. Demonstrate an appropriate warm-up and warm-down routine using all the main muscle groups. Explain why both routines are important. Examples of suitable warm up activities include: skipping, running on the spot, stretching both arms high above the head and then relaxing down, bending the knees and dropping the head, rolling the head slowly around tensing and relaxing the shoulders.

2. Discuss the safety rules associated with athletics, particularly throwing and jumping events. Explain the most appropriate clothing to wear

3. Take part in six events at least one from each section, improving your distance or time over a number of attempts.

Field events

- Discus
- Shot put
- Throwing a cricket ball
- Javelin
- High jump
- Long jump
- Standing jump
- Sargent jump (to have a diagram)

Track events

- 100m
- 200m
- 400m
- 800m
- 1500m
- 100m hurdles

Team events

- 4 x 100m relay
- Team assault course
- Assisted blindfold race

4. Find out and explain to a leader how to further take part in athletics in your local area

Note

- This badge is awarded for participation and putting in your best effort.

- For the high jump, special attention must be given to the nature of the jump, and the landing facilities required. Unless expert tuition and supervision is available, you must not attempt the Fosbury Flop. The scissor jump is a more accessible method

- The recommended weights of the shot, discus and cricket ball are 2.73 kg, 1kg and 0.135kg respectively.

→ ATHLETICS PLUS ACTIVITY BADGE

Complete the requirements below:

1. Hold the Scout Athletics Badge

2. To gain this badge, Scouts must complete the requirements below:

- Demonstrate an appropriate warm-up and warm-down routine using all the main muscle groups. Explain why both routines are important.

- Discuss the safety rules associated with athletics, particularly throwing and jumping events.

- Compete in any three events (two track and one field, or vice versa) and gain points as indicated on the score chart below.

→ BASIC AVIATION SKILLS

Complete the requirements below:

1. Know the rules relating to access to airfields in *Policy, Organisation and Rules*. Draw a diagram/map or make a model of an airfield to show and name the different areas.

2. Understand the terms: nose, fuselage, tail, main-plane, port and starboard. Know the names of the control surfaces of an aircraft.

3. Construct and fly a chuck glider for at least five seconds or build and fly a hot-air balloon or kite.

4. Choose one of the following activities:

a. Collect photographs or pictures of six aircraft that interest you, name them and their operational uses.

b. Discuss an airline that you are interested in, or have travelled on, showing pictures of aircraft livery and logos.

5. Take part in a Patrol or Troop visit with other Scouts to a place of aviation interest.

6. From the list of Aviation Skills Training Activities on the opposite page, complete four items, each to be taken from a different section.

→ AVIATION SKILLS

Complete the requirements below:

1. Qualify with one of the following:

a. Hold the Basic Aviation Skills Badge.

b. Be at least 11½ years and complete requirements 1 and 5 of the Basic Aviation Skills Badge.

2. List the main types of aircraft and identify the parts of an aeroplane.

3. Identify 12 aircraft in use today from pictures or in flight. These must include at least two civil commercial aircraft, two military aircraft and two light private aircraft.

4. Explain how wind speed and direction are measured and how weather can affect various air activities. Demonstrate how to obtain a local forecast for an air activity.

5. Understand the phonetic alphabet, explain why it is used and demonstrate its use.

6. Demonstrate ability to trim a suitable model glider to perform a straight glide, stall and specified turn. Explain the relationships between lift, drag, thrust and weight.

7. Choose one of the following activities:

a. Fly in a light aircraft or glider as a passenger and know the rules in *Policy, Organisation and Rules* relating to flying.

b. Help to organise a visit to an airfield or place of aviation history for a group of Scouts. Explain to your assessor what you would need to tell the Scouts prior to the visit.

8. From the list of Aviation Skills Training Activities complete a further six items taken from at least four different sections.

→ ADVANCED AVIATION SKILLS

Complete the requirements below:

1. Qualify with one of the following:

a. Hold the Aviation Skills Badge.

b. Be at least 13 years old and complete requirements 1 and 4 of the Aviation Skills Badge.

2. Name the main control surfaces of an aeroplane; explain how they work and how they are controlled.

3. Choose one of the following two activities:

a. Explain the duties of an aircraft marshaller and demonstrate marshalling signals.

b. Explain the duties of a crew leader for a glider launch and demonstrate procedure and signals.

4. Know the types of air maps and the conventional signs used on them.

5. Choose one of the following activities:

a. Explain the basic principles of a piston engine, including the four-stroke cycle, with consideration of valve and ignition timing.

b. Compare and contrast the main parts and workings of a piston engine and a jet engine.

6. Explain the difference between ground speed and air speed and how wind is used in take off and landing. Explain how a wing gives lift. Explain the causes of stalling.

7. Take part in an air experience flight and point out on an air map the features that are flown over. Choose any means of air travel, for example powered aircraft, glider, balloon, airship.

8. From the list of Aviation Skills Training Activities complete another six items from at least four different sections.

→ AVIATION SKILLS TRAINING ACTIVITIES

Section 1 - Practical skills

1. Build and fly one of the following:

a. A rubber-powered model for at least 15 seconds

b. A glider for at least 15 seconds

c. A model airship

d. A hovercraft

e. A boomerang

2. Build a scale model aircraft to a satisfactory standard from one of the following:

a. Plastic kit, plans or photographs. Talk about the aircraft's key points and history.

b. By modifying a standard kit, produce a different but authentic version of the aircraft.

3. Make a solid model where all control surfaces operate and can be used to demonstrate their effect.

4. Demonstrate the signals required to launch a manned glider and participate as part of a launch or recovery crew.

5. Arrange for a suitably experienced instructor to give training in how a parachute works. Be able to put on a parachute harness and demonstrate the correct landing roll.

6. Assist with the launching and recovery of a paraglider. Make two ascents, without release.

7. Know the rules in *Policy, Organisation and Rules* relating to flying and fly in an aircraft as a passenger.

8. Undertake a project to demonstrate a particular aeronautical principle and build a suitable model to illustrate it.

9. Build and fly at least five different designs of paper aeroplane, using published plans if desired.

10. One other activity of a similar nature and level of achievement as agreed by your leadership team.

Section 2 - Flight safety and airmanship

1. Know the dangers posed to aircraft by birds and other wildlife and the methods employed to reduce the problem.

2. Understand the working of an airport fire service or emergency team, the equipment employed and main rescue methods.

3. Know the reasons for airport security, the main threats and means of countering these threats.

4. Explain how an aircraft lifejacket works. Demonstrate its use.

5. Draw a runway and its circuit patterns indicating:

a. climb-out; cross wind; down wind; base leg; final leg

b. runway markings

c. taxi-ways; over-shoot; under-shoot areas.

6. Explain and illustrate the purpose and workings of an ejector seat.

7. Understand the physical fitness requirements to fly as a pilot or passenger. Be aware of health concerns such as ear blockage, hypoxia and deep vein thrombosis.

8. Explain the emergency procedures for a manned glider in flight in the case of:

a. cable failure in a winch or aero-tow launch, and engine failure of a motor glider

b. structural failure or collision at altitude

c. inability to release cable in the case of winch launch or aero-tow.

d. Altitude loss to the extent that safe soaring is no longer feasible.

9. Understand the responsibilities of the commander of an aircraft. Examples include briefings, safety of load and passengers, completing relevant paperwork.

10. Demonstrate pre-flight inspection of an aircraft and explain why inspection of each part is important to safe operation.

11. One other activity of a similar nature and level of achievement as agreed by the leadership team.

Section 3 - Aerospace operations

1. Describe at least six airlines by their names and markings, completing one of the following:

a. Identify the home countries and main operating bases.

b. Describe six routes operated by each airline, together with the aircraft used.

c. Describe the operations of an all-cargo airline. Know the main types of cargo aircraft and their special applications.

2. Discuss the design characteristics of a chosen aircraft in relation to its operational role.

3. Understand the principles of air launched and ground based anti-aircraft weapons and the systems used to counteract them.

4. Demonstrate knowledge of air and space surveillance systems, their types and applications.

5. Understand the advantages of mid-air refuelling for military aircraft, the main methods of fuel transfer and the main types of tanker used.

6. Discuss the problem of aerospace flight including acceleration to escape velocity, the reason for weightlessness and re-entry problems.

7. Demonstrate a general knowledge of the progress of space exploration, describing in particular one space programme.

8. Understand the principles of re-usable space vehicles. Know their advantages and disadvantages over conventional rocket systems/launch vehicles.

9. Explain the roles of two recent space probes and two recently launched satellites, giving the main types of instruments used.

10. Demonstrate the scale of the solar system with a drawing or model to show the relative positions of the planets.

11. Any other one activity of a similar nature and level of achievement as agreed by the leadership team.

Section 4 - Navigation

1. Explain the workings and potential errors of an aircraft compass.

2. For a cross-country flight of at least 80 kilometres, work out the time of flight from an overhead starting point to an overhead destination for a given airspeed, assuming i. a given headwind; ii. a given tailwind.

3. Explain the workings of a Global Positioning System (GPS) and be able to demonstrate its usage.

4. Explain the workings of aircraft pressure instruments, for example an altimeter or air speed indicator. Explain the sources of errors.

5. For a cross-country flight of at least 80 kilometres, determine a heading given a track, wind speed and direction.

6. Demonstrate knowledge of conventional symbols used on an aeronautical chart and show how to do simple flight calculations.

7. Illustrate latitude and longitude by simple diagrams. Explain the need for different types of map projections.

8. Show a basic knowledge of Aeronav aids and equipment. Understand the concept of GPS.

9. Any other one activity of a similar nature and level of achievement as agreed by the Section leadership team.

Section 5 - Meteorology

1. Identify the basic clouds and explain how they are formed.

2. Explain how wind speed is measured and how weather can affect various air activities.

3. Demonstrate how to get a local forecast for an air activity.

4. Explain the flight conditions that can be expected in various cloud formations and weather conditions.

5. Outline how temperature and pressure are measured, list the units used and demonstrate conversions between different units by use of tables and by calculation.

6. Identify the weather conditions associated with the movement of air masses over the United Kingdom for example Polar, Tropical, Maritime, and Continental.

7. Explain how readings of upper air conditions are obtained.

8. Collect detailed weather maps of the United Kingdom either from the Internet or from a newspaper for a two-week period. Illustrate the development of significant weather features over this period.

9. Be able to interpret Met Office reports and forecasts for pilots, such as METAR and TAF.

10. Any other one activity of a similar nature and level of achievement as agreed by the Section leadership team.

Section 6 - Aero engines

1. Explain how jets or rockets obtain thrust. Explain the principle of the ramjet. Explain the principles of a centrifugal or axial compressor type jet engine and identify the main components of such an engine.

2. Discuss the relative merits of piston engines, turbojets, turboprops, turbofans, ramjets and rockets.

3. Identify the main types of aircraft fuels and fuel systems.

4. Demonstrate knowledge of the causes of aircraft noise and disturbance. Know the design methods used to reduce aircraft noise and how the effects on local communities can be reduced.

5. Demonstrate knowledge of the effect of aircraft engine emissions on the atmosphere and how these can be reduced.

6. Any other one activity of a similar nature and level of achievement as agreed by the Section leadership team.

Section 7 - Communications and Air Traffic Control

1. Identify the signals used on an airfield signals square, together with runway and airfield markings.

2. Identify the lamp and pyrotechnic signals used on an airfield.

3. Understand why Morse code is still transmitted by navigational beacons and be able to recognise six three-letter sequences either from a recording or written copy.

4. Explain the system of air traffic control in use at a small civilian airfield.

5. Demonstrate examples of the ground-to-air emergency code.

6. Understand the special communications difficulties for activities such as paragliding or hang gliding and the need for clearance in areas of military flying.

7. Any other one activity of a similar nature and level of achievement as agreed by your leadership team.

Section 8 - Principles of flight

1. Explain the meaning of trim and the importance of weight and balance.

2. Explain the purpose and operation of flaps, slots and slats.

3. Explain how basic aerobatic manoeuvres are carried out.

4. Demonstrate knowledge of the principles of take-off and landing with special reference to light aircraft.

5. Explain the methods by which short or vertical take-off can be achieved.

6. Describe the airflow around a modern square parachute, explaining how it develops lift and how it is controlled.

7. Attain a reasonable standard on a home computer flight simulator programme and understand why the aircraft behaves as it does. The suitability of the programme is to be agreed by the Section leadership team.

8. Show knowledge of the methods for operating specialised passenger aircraft into city centres such as helicopters, STOL, tilt wing etc and the main drawbacks.

9. Any other one activity of a similar nature and level of achievement as agreed by your leadership team.

→ **CAMP COOK**

Complete the requirements below:

1. Explain how and where to shop for food and how to transport it.

2. Demonstrate proper storage and cooking under camp conditions. This must include knowledge of hygiene in the camp kitchen and how to prevent food poisoning.

3. Devise a day's menu (including quantities) for a group of four to six Scouts. (Consider first any cultural, religious, vegetarian or dietary needs of the group).

4. Successfully cook and serve the day's menu.

Note: All dishes are to be cooked under camp conditions and preferably on a wood fire.

→ **CAMPER**

Complete the requirements below:

1. Camp under canvas* as a Scout for at least 15 nights.

2. Lead a group of Scouts in the pitching, striking and packing of a four to six person tent.

3. Know what to look for when choosing a campsite and in deciding the best position to pitch tents.

4. Show an understanding of the reasons for hygiene and the importance of being safe and tidy in camp.

5. Demonstrate how to store food hygienically at camp.

6. Construct two useful camp gadgets such as a camp larder, altar fire, flagpole, camp gate etc.

7. Prepare and cook either a full hot breakfast or a main meal for four to six people.

* under canvas refers to any tentage

→ **CAMPSITE SERVICE**

Complete the requirements below:

1. Hold the Camper Badge.

2. Have worked for at least two days at a permanent District, County/Area or National Scout campsite or similar Activity Centre, helping the warden or manager to their satisfaction.

3. Explain and where possible demonstrate the maintenance required for some campsite equipment.

4. Explain and where possible demonstrate four of the following:

a. The reasons for having clean toilets

b. How to unblock a drain

c. The prevention of frozen pipes and the steps to be taken when over ground pipes burst or leak

d. The need for good site drainage and clear ditches

e. Refuse disposal, including how to maximise the retention of recyclable materials

f. Respect for wildlife, balancing the requirements of campers

g. The use of computers in campsite management

h. Other important tasks as identified by the Warden or Manager.

5. Become familiar with an activity run on site. Explain the use and maintenance of equipment used for that activity.

6. Demonstrate an ability to competently use three items of equipment appropriate to your role.

7. Discuss developments and improvements you would like to see at a permanent campsite with which you are familiar.

→ CAVER

Complete the requirements below:

1. Take part in at least four trips to at least two different cave systems. (Each visit must be as a member of a properly led group).

2. Keep a record of these trips and the routes followed.

3. Have a good knowledge of the contents of the caving and cave conservation codes, and be able to show to the assessor an awareness of the environmental issues around caving.

Note: Reference should be made to the Activity Rules in chapter nine of *Policy, Organisation and Rules* and the Adventurous Activity Permit Scheme.

→ CHEF

Complete the requirements below:

1. Discuss how and where to shop for food and how to transport it.

2. Demonstrate proper storage and cooking. This should include knowledge of hygiene in the kitchen and how to prevent food poisoning.

3. Create a menu for a three-course meal for between two to four people to include the following menu items:

   - two cooked dishes

   - a cake or pastry dish

   - two sauces such as Mornay, apple, curry, mustard, parsley, chocolate, custard etc.

4. Cook and serve this menu, demonstrating the necessary preparation and serving skills.

5. Plan a full balanced menu for a small group of Scouts for at least one weekend. Discuss the choices made, assuming full kitchen facilities are available.

→ CIRCUS SKILLS

Complete the requirements below:

1. Select one skill from any two of the five alternatives below. Under experienced guidance, show by continuing effort some achievement in the two selected skills. Demonstrate the two selected skills before an audience.

a. **Aerial:** Trapeze, Roman rings, aerial ladder, aerial rope, wire walking or related skills.

b. **Balance:** Trick-cycling, stilts, ladder, tightrope, wire walking, perch, roller bolo, slack-rope.

c. **Manipulative:** Plate spinning, cigar boxes, club swinging, devil sticks, diablo sticks, juggling.

d. **Ground:** Handstands, tumbling, acrobatics

e. **Clowning:** Including make-up and costume.

2. Find out about aspects of circus life, and discuss these with an adult.

3. Observe at least two circus or street performers events and discuss these.

Note: Before attempting any of the skills, participants must be of a fitness standard appropriate to both enjoy and execute the skill. Instructions in the safe use of the equipment must be given and all safety precautions and procedures must be observed in line with the Association's Safety Policy. Participants are encouraged to join a workshop, or other course, to learn their chosen skills.

→ CLIMBER

Complete the requirements below:

1. Show knowledge of the rope types used for rock climbing and explain how to coil and maintain them.

2. Demonstrate the ability to fit a climbing harness and tie in correctly.

3. Show an understanding of the calls used in climbing.

4. Demonstrate the ability to abseil down a face (typically not less than 10 metres).

5. Take part in four separate climbs of up to 'Difficult' standard each using a different route. An experienced climber must supervise the climbs and will evaluate competence.

6. Explain the safety rules for climbing on both natural and artificial rock faces.

7. Show an awareness of the environmental issues around climbing on natural rock faces.

Note: Reference should be made to the Activity Rules in chapter nine of *Policy, Organisation and Rules* and the Adventurous Activity Permit Scheme.

There is no requirement for the Scout to lead the rock climbs, only to be a competent second. Wherever possible, natural rock-face should be used.

→ COMMUNICATOR

Complete the requirements in any one of the following alternatives:

Alternative A - Radio communication

1. Complete the following three tasks:

- Log 25 different amateur radio stations, showing date, time, call sign, frequency, readability and location. Some broadcast stations may be included.

- Demonstrate how to tune a simple communications receiver.

- Give an example of a typical 'greetings' message.

2. Explain in simple terms how radio waves travel around the world. Know the more commonly used HF and VHF amateur frequency bands.

3. Complete the following two tasks:

- Know the Phonetic Alphabet and define at least eight international Q code signals.

- Demonstrate your ability to recognise call signs from the UK and near continent.

4. Visit an amateur radio station.

5. Understand the regulations governing the use of amateur radio equipment.

Note: A Scout who holds or gains an Amateur Radio Licence (Foundation, Intermediate or Full) or the Marine Radio Operator's Certificate of Competence and Authority to Operate or the Flight Radio Telephone Operator's Licence automatically qualifies for this badge.

Alternative B - Communication codes

1. Send and receive a short message by Morse code or Semaphore at a rate of five words per minute.

2. When sending and receiving a message, demonstrate that you know the appropriate procedure.

3. Know the International Phonetic Alphabet and define at least eight international Q code signals.

4. Construct a simple Morse code oscillator and send a short message.

Alternative C - Mobile and Internet communication

1. Know how to use your mobile safely and how to keep it safe.

2. Understand the meaning of the following terms: SMS, MMS, 3G, WAP, Bluetooth.

3. Send a creative text, multi-media or video message to invite a friend to a Scout event.

4. Manage a mobile phone address book, including setting up groups.

5. Show you can accurately input text at a rate of 50 characters per minute.

6. Know how to keep yourself safe when chatting online.

7. Know how to use an instant messaging service such as MSN Messenger or AOL Instant Messenger.

8. Show you know the meaning of some popular chat abbreviations.

9. Send a creative and imaginative email or instant message to a friend showing photos of an enjoyable Scouting activity you have been involved with.

10. Manage an email address book, including setting up groups.

Note: There are many online articles that can help in supporting this badge, for example:

Keep Safe Online (www.chatdanger.com); www.thinkuknow.co.uk and The National Mobile Phone Crime Unit (www.met.police.uk/mobilephone/index.htm).

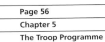

→ CRAFT

Complete the requirements below:

1. Make or decorate one or more articles, using whenever possible, original design ideas. The project should be discussed beforehand with a member of the leadership team and should take around six hours to complete. Appropriate care must be taken with all tools and materials to avoid injury. Some example projects are as follows:

   - Make a container using basket-making, woodturning, pottery, embroidery on plastic canvas, glass blowing, fibreglass construction.

   - Make a belt, bag, wall hanging, tablemat or waistcoat by weaving, macramé, beadwork or from leather.

   - Make an item of clothing or soft furnishing by sewing or knitting. (You may follow a pattern).

   - Decorate clothing or soft furnishing (cushion, tablecloth etc. using embroidery, tapestry, lace making, tie and dye or wax and dye or fabric paints.

   - Make a picture using techniques such as mosaic, staining glass, quilting, calligraphy, pyrography, pressed flowers, fabric collage, printing with potato, lino, string, drypoint, aquatint, silk screen or similar. Decorate an article (wood, metal, glass etc. by engraving or etching; or decorate enamelware).

   - Make an ornament or decorative article using candle-making, arranging flowers, carving in any medium (e.g. wood, slate, stone, soap), fly tying, jewellery making, pewterwork, copper or silver smithing, stone polishing, stone masonry or sculpture.

   - Make a small item of furniture.

   - Decorate a cake for a special occasion.

   - Any other project of a similar skill level as agreed beforehand with the leadership team.

→ CYCLIST

To gain this badge, Scouts must complete the requirements below:

1. Use a bicycle that is properly equipped and kept in good working order for at least six months.

2. Demonstrate an ability to carry out essential maintenance and repairs, including the following:

   a. Check and adjust the brakes.

   b. Check and adjust the gear change.

   c. Adjust the seat and handlebars to a correct height.

   d. Remove a wheel and locate and repair a puncture.

   e. Check and adjust your cycle helmet.

   f. Maintain a set of lights.

3. Complete the requirements in one of the following alternatives:

Alternative A

1. Explain what extra precautions should be taken when cycling in the dark or in wet weather. Understand why motor vehicles take longer to stop in the wet.

2. Have a basic knowledge of first aid and what to do in case of accidents.

3. Have a working knowledge of map reading. Be able to orientate a map using a compass or conspicuous features. Be able to estimate distances and times taken to travel.

4. Plan and carry out an all day cycle ride of not less than 40 kilometres (25 miles).

Either: demonstrate an ability to control a cycle along a slalom course, show an understanding of the Highway Code (including road signs and helmet use), or gain Bikeability Level 2 or 3.

Alternative B - Off road

1. Have an understanding of The Scout Association's rules for taking part in adventurous activities.

2. Demonstrate an understanding of the Mountain Bike Code of Conduct.

3. Demonstrate the ability to control the cycle over different types of terrain.

4. Show an understanding of the damage that may be caused to the environment through careless cycling across the countryside.

5. Have a basic knowledge of first aid, including the treatment of hypothermia and know what to do in the case of an accident.

6. Have a working knowledge of map reading. Be able to orientate a map using a compass or conspicuous features. Be able to estimate distances and times taken to travel.

7. Plan and carry out an all day ride of not less than 30 kilometres (20 miles) on unpaved tracks.

Alternative C - Cycle tricks

Achieve the Gold Trix Award of the British Schools Cycling Association.

Alternative D

Achieve the Level 3 Go-MTB Award of Scottish Cycling.

→ **DINGHY SAILOR**

Complete the requirements below:

Qualify for the Start Sailing Stage 2 Award of the Royal Yachting Association's Young Sailors Scheme.

Note: Reference should be made to the Activity Rules in chapter nine of *Policy, Organisation and Rules* and the Adventurous Activity Permit Scheme.

Web: www.rya.org.uk

→ **D.I.Y**

Complete the requirements below:

1. Be able to work safely in the home minimising dangers to yourself and others; covering the following:

a. Recognise hazard symbols and signs (e.g. toxic, flammable, irritant, electrical danger, slippery surface).

b. Know about and use safety equipment (e.g. goggles, gloves, masks, ear defenders).

c. Know how and where to turn off main supplies (water, electricity, gas) to the house. Know how to isolate individual electrical circuits at the consumer unit.

2. Show or explain how you would deal with four DIY emergencies from the list below:

a. Unblocking a sink

b. Renewing a tap washer

c. Curing an airlock in water or radiator pipes

d. Thawing frozen pipes

e. Patching a leaking pipe

f. Adjusting the float arm of a cistern

g. Fitting a fused electrical plug to a cable

h. Replacing a mains fuse or resetting a mains circuit breaker

i. Changing a light bulb

j. Helping to repair a broken window

k. Repairing a tear in clothes or upholstery

l. Removing common stains e.g. ink, wine, and coffee.

3. Take an active part in two major DIY projects, indoors or out, such as:

a. Insulate a loft and/or fit draught proofing to windows and doors.

b. Insulate a cold-water storage tank, pipes and hot water cylinder.

c. Plan a colour scheme for a room and prepare a sample board.

d. Prepare and paint, paper or tile the walls of a room.

e. Prepare and paint woodwork or furniture.

f. Fit a curtain track and hang curtains.

g. Make a freestanding storage unit or put up shelves.

h. Cover a floor with vinyl overlay, lino, tiles or carpet.

i. Hang a door and fit or repair locks and oher door furniture.

j. Carry out a home security survey and take action to make the house more secure by fitting window locks, marking property with a UV pen, or fitting a burglar alarm.

k. Lay a patio or path.

l. Build a low wall, barbecue, gate or fence.

m. Create and maintain a garden pond.

n. Repair bodywork on a car and clean and polish the car.

o. Any other project(s) of a similar skill level as agreed with an adult.

Note: The Scout should be made aware that there are regulations that limit what an amateur may do in the home. Adult supervision is required for many of these projects.

→ DRAGON BOATING

Complete the requirements below:

1. Understand the safety rules, capsize drill and the water buddy system.
2. Know the procedures for loading, numbering off, stopping, bracing the boat, forward and backward paddling.
3. Understand the instructions and commands as advised by The Dragon Boat Racing Association.
4. Carry out practice training sessions for a minimum of two hours. Practise a race over a distance of at least 250 metres.
5. Take part in a competitive or timed dragon boat event over a course of at least 250 metres.

Where a Dragon Boat is unavailable the badge may be taken in a Bell Boat

Note: Reference should be made to the Activity Rules in chapter nine of *Policy, Organisation and Rules* and the Adventurous Activity Permit Scheme.

→ ELECTRONICS

Complete the requirements below:

1. Show an understanding of components by completing the following three tasks:

a. Be able to recognise common electronic components that are shown to you. Explain, in simple terms, the functions they perform in electronic circuits.

b. Understand the systems used for marking components with their values and be able to identify the values of resistors and capacitors so marked. Understand the importance of the rating of a component.

c. Know the symbols that are used to represent common components in circuit diagrams. Show how to identify the polarity of a diode and a specific pin number on an integrated circuit.

2. Demonstrate knowledge of safe working practices to be followed when handling electronic components, and circuit boards and when undertaking soldering.

3. Use a multimeter to measure voltage, current and resistance in a simple circuit. Discuss the relationship between these values.

4. Discuss the main differences in operation of digital and analogue circuits.

5. Construct three simple circuits, one of which should be based mainly on digital electronics. These may be from a book or magazine, or circuits that you have designed yourself. At least one of the circuits should be soldered using either strip-board or a custom made printed circuit board. Explain the principles behind the operation of each circuit and the typical values of voltage and current found in each.

→ ENTERTAINER

As part of a group of Scouts, complete all the requirements in one of the following alternatives:

Alternative A

1. Write and plan an original entertainment. This could take the form of a sketch, film or slide and tape presentation, campfire or stage routine involving the following: mime, drama, music, storytelling, conjuring, photography or sound recording.
2. Prepare the entertainment, ensuring that everyone has a job to do, for example actor, producer, stage manager, front of house, publicity manager.
3. Present the entertainment to an audience at a school, Pack, Troop or parents' evening.

Alternative B

1. Take an active part in a Scout Show or other production. This should require a commitment to regular rehearsals.

→ EQUESTRIAN

Complete the requirements below:

Riding

1. Be able to catch a pony from a field or stable and tack up for riding.

2. Be able to walk, trot and canter a pony.

3. Be able to jump over small fences.

Grooming and care

4. Be able to groom correctly and explain why this is necessary.

5. Know how to take care of saddlery and other equipment.

Horse health

6. Understand some of the basic health issues affecting horses, including worming and laminitis.

7. Show a basic knowledge of grass management to include recognising poisonous plants and the results of overgrazing.

Safety

8. Discuss road safety for riding.

9. Explain why a hat, body protector and stirrup and other safety equipment is necessary.

→ FIRE SAFETY

Complete the requirements below:

1. Understand how the local Fire Service is organised.

2. Explain what action should be taken and why on discovering the outbreak of a fire in the home or at camp.

3. Give an explanation of the process of combustion. Know the effects of smoke and heat, and how to act in smoke.

4. Know the dangers and fire precautions necessary in the home relating to:

a. oil heaters and open solid fuel fires

b. portable electric fires

c. drying clothes

d. electric wiring and fuses

e. smoking materials particularly matches

f. uses of household gas

g. party decorations, candles

h. closing doors and windows.

5. Explain the benefits of installed smoke detectors and describe where they should be sited.

6. Know the dangers of fire at camp and what precautions should be taken.

7. Know the causes of heath and grass fires.

8. Know how to make an emergency call for the Fire Service.

9. Be able to recognise various fire extinguishers including water, dry powder, foam and carbon dioxide types. Know what kinds of fire they should be used on.

10. Know how to deal with a person whose clothes are on fire.

11. Talk with your family about the actions to be taken in the event of a fire at home.

Note: Taking part in a locally organised course with the Fire and Rescue Service will enable you to complete this badge.

→ FORESTER

Complete the requirements below:

1. Be able to identify at least eight common types of tree growing in your area, including both deciduous and coniferous.

2. Know how to identify trees using identification keys.

3. Prepare soil and successfully transplant a young tree.

4. Understand the management of both natural woodland and commercial forests. Know the damage to which these areas may be exposed, for example through wind, frost, fire and animals.

5. Show how to select, use and care for appropriate equipment, and know the safety issues involved.

6. Show how to fell and trim out a tree or know the principles of laying a hedge.

Note: The correct use of axes and saws must be understood and training given by a skilled person. Supervision by an adult is essential.

→ GLOBAL CONSERVATION

Complete the requirements below:

1. Find out about an environmental issue that is important to your local community. Examples include:

   - recycling

   - energy efficiency in the home

   - water conservation

   - local conservation groups

   - water or air pollution.

2. Take part in a Troop activity that improves local conservation. Examples include:

   - recycling

   - wildlife

   - energy

   - pollution

   - traffic fumes.

The activity should involve at least five sessions over some weeks or a more concentrated project done over a shorter period of time, perhaps at a weekend conservation camp.

3. Get involved in a campaign to make others aware of an environmental issue. Examples might include the following:

   - Writing to your MP or other local agency about it

   - Use of an original, eye-catching method to inform others about saving energy or resources

   - Speaking to a community group

   - Recycling printer cartridges, tools or spectacles etc to aid an overseas development project.

→ GUIDE

Complete the requirements in one of the following alternatives:

Alternative A – for rural and suburban areas

1. Show that you know the locality around either your home or Scout Meeting Place up to a radius of two kilometres in urban Districts and three kilometres in rural Districts. This should include knowledge of the location of many of the following:

a. Doctors, veterinary surgeons, dentists, hospitals, ambulance station

b. Fire station, police station, garages, shopping centres, retail parks and convenience stores

c. Main bus stops, railway stations and routes of buses and trains to surrounding areas

d. Local Scout Meeting Places, public parks, theatres, sports and leisure complexes, cinemas, places of worship, museums, schools, colleges and local government buildings

e. Local routes that give access to the nearest motorway or national routes.

2. Show how to use a street map to point out six locations from requirement 1. From your home or Scout Meeting Place, show the quickest route to one of the places.

Alternative B - for urban areas

1. Have a general knowledge of what parts of the country are served from the local airport, and from the local mainline railway and coach stations.

2. Know how to reach the local airport, mainline railway and coach stations and major tourist attractions from your Scout Meeting Place or home.

3. Show how to use a map of your District. Use it to point out six examples of places of interest. Show how to get to these places from your Scout Meeting Place or home.

4. Give clear directions to a place of interest eight kilometres away to a person travelling by car or public transport.

5. Have a knowledge of which major local roads link to the motorway and A road network, and of the main cities the latter serve.

Note: The Troop leadership team may at its discretion vary the area described in requirement 1.

→ HERITAGE

Complete the requirements in one of the following alternatives:

Alternative A

1. Over an agreed period, be involved with others in a project, which helps preserve some aspect of national or local heritage.

Examples include projects involving a steam railway, bell ringing, archaeology, local history, historic monument or building, museum.

Alternative B

1. Over an agreed period, be involved with a group that keeps traditional entertainment alive. Take part in at least one public performance.

Examples include country or folk dancing, puppet show, folk singing, re-enactment, a musical group or band.

Alternative C

1. Complete a study of an aspect of national or local history or of family heritage.

2. Display, exhibit or present the results in a library, to a group of Scouts or local interest group.

→ HIKER

Complete the requirements below:

1. As a member of a group of at least four and not more than seven Scouts, carry out three expeditions or journeys as follows:

a. A journey or expedition of at least 12 km

b. Two journeys or expeditions of at least 20 km, both to include an overnight stop.

2. Before undertaking each expedition or journey, the group must provide a detailed Route Plan (see Factsheet FS 120409).

3. All members of the group must show that they know the intended route and have knowledge of basic navigation, First Aid and emergency procedures.

4. After each journey or expedition, the group should give a verbal report.

5. Demonstrate awareness of developments in technology, such as the Global Positioning System (GPS); digital mapping; waterproof maps etc.

Note: Reference should be made to the Activity Rules in chapter nine of *Policy, Organisation and Rules* and the Adventurous Activity Permit Scheme and the Nights Away Permit Scheme. Expeditions by canoe, horseback or cycle of similar duration may be acceptable provided at least one overnight journey or expedition on foot is carried out. During cycling activities, cycle helmets must be worn at all times.

The distances stated may be varied at the Leader's discretion. Alternative activities may be carried out as agreed by the leadership team.

Factsheet FS 120409 (Route Plan) is available from the Scout Information Centre.

→ HILL WALKER

Complete the requirements below:

1. With others, plan at least five one day journeys of 14km or more in hilly country. At least three of these are to be in areas defined as Terrain One, led by an appropriate Permit Holder.

2. Using Ordnance Survey maps, complete all the information required on a Route Plan for each journey (see Factsheet FS 120409).

3. Before setting out, list and explain the use of the equipment that should be taken including:

a. Spare food, and safety/emergency equipment

b. What should be worn

c. What should be carried

4. Over a period, complete the planned journeys. Take turns in leading the group for part of the time.

5. Make a report to an audience about at least one of your journeys. Route cards, sketch maps and photographs should be presented where possible. Demonstrate how the map and compass was used during the journey.

6. Demonstrate how the map and compass were used during come of the journeys.

7. Demonstrate an awareness of the need to preserve the natural environment. For example, avoiding erosion, conserving wildlife habitat.

8. Demonstrate awareness of developments in technology, such as the Global Positioning System (GPS): digital mapping; waterproof maps etc.

9. Show knowledge of the publication Safety on Mountains (British Mountaineering Council).

Note: Reference should be made to the Activity Rules in chapter nine of *Policy, Organisation and Rules* and the Adventurous Activity Permit Scheme

→ HOBBIES

Complete the requirements for one of the following alternatives:

Alternative A

1. Take up a hobby or interest for which you do not already have an Activity Badge.

2. Keep a record of involvement for a period agreed with a member of the leadership team.

Alternative B

1. Make a collection or study of objects over an agreed period. Examples are stamps, metal badges, teaspoons or bookmarks.

2. Talk to a group about the collection or study chosen. Explain the reason for the choice.

Note: This badge is designed for those who have a regular hobby for which there is no specific Activity Badge. You can gain more than one Hobbies Badge. Alternative requirements can be agreed with a member of the Troop leadership team.

→ INTERPRETER

Complete the requirements in one of the following alternatives:

Alternative A

Complete the following in any foreign language:

1. Carry on a simple conversation for about ten minutes.

2. Write a letter of around 150 words.

3. After a few minutes of study, give a translation of a paragraph of basic text.

4. Act as an interpreter for a visitor who does not speak in your native language.

5. Communicate with a person who does not speak your native language.

Alternative B

Complete the following requirements in a recognised sign language such as Makaton or British Sign Language.

1. Carry out a simple conversation for about ten minutes.

2. Use sign language to describe a Scouting experience to another person.

3. Act as a translator for a short conversation between a sign language user and someone with no sign language experience.

4. Invite a sign language user to talk to the Troop about what it is like to have hearing or speech impediments. Help by acting as translator for them during their visit.

→ LIBRARIAN

Complete the requirements below:

1. Demonstrate that you know how to look after books and CD-ROMs.

2. Show that you know how to use a library catalogue.

3. Explain how fiction and non-fiction books are arranged on the shelves and why they are treated differently.

4. Know what is meant by a reference book or material. Gather information you need for a journey with a purpose by using some of the following reference material: leisure leaflet; bus or train timetable; almanac; gazetteer, Yellow Pages; Who's Who?

5. Demonstrate how to search for information on a CD-ROM encyclopaedia or using the Internet.

6. Talk to the assessor about either:

a. books you have read and why you enjoyed them; or

b. information you have researched from books or online which you have found of particular interest.

→ LIFESAVER

Complete the requirements below:

1. Understand and explain how you would effect a rescue from water using the following methods: reach, throw, wade, row.

2. Hold one of the following:

a. Royal Lifesaving Society UK Rookie Lifeguard – Junior Lifesaving

b. Royal Lifesaving Society UK Lifesaving 3 Award

c. National Aquatic Rescue Standard Silver Cross.

3. Explain and where possible demonstrate actions to take in the following cases:

a. Someone falling through ice

b. House fire

c. Gas leak

d. Car accident

e. Someone who has touched a live wire.

Show an understanding of the dangers associated with each method of rescue.

→ MARTIAL ARTS

Complete the requirements below:

1. Attend regular training sessions in the chosen activity for not less than six months and demonstrate an improvement of at least one level over that period.

2. Take part in a competition or demonstration and discuss your performance with an instructor.

Note: Reference should be made to *Policy, Organisation and Rules* relating to Martial Arts.

→ MASTER AT ARMS

Complete the requirements below:

1. Attend regular training sessions in a chosen activity (fencing, shooting or archery) and demonstrate an improvement in skill. Training should be for at least five sessions.

2. Know the safety rules associated with the activity and demonstrate their use.

3. Take part in the chosen activity at an officially supervised contest and discuss performance with the instructor.

Note: Reference must be made to the activity rules in *Policy, Organisation and Rules* relating to Shooting and Archery.

→ MECHANIC

Complete the requirements in one of the following alternatives:

Alternative A – motor car

1. Know the principles of operation of an internal combustion engine and understand the function of the clutch, gearbox and rear axle differential.

2. Show how to check and refill the windscreen wash bottle of a car.

3. Show how to change a bulb at the front and in the rear light cluster of a car.

4. Show how to check the level of water in the radiator, 'top up' the radiator and know the importance of anti-freeze.

5. Show how to check tyre pressures and inflate a tyre correctly.

6. Remove and replace a road wheel.

7. Explain what to look for when checking that a tyre conforms to the legal requirement. Understand the reason why cross and radial ply tyres should not be mixed on the same axle.

8. Show how to change a wiper blade.

9. Know the outline requirements for an MOT road test.

Alternative B - power boat

1. Complete one from the following two activities:

a. Be able to discuss the principles and performance of several types of motorboat engines, other than two-stroke. Show knowledge of the maintenance needed by a familiar type of marine internal combustion engine, other than two-stroke.

b. Assist with the maintenance, dismantle, service and re-assemble an outboard engine. Demonstrate proper fitting to the transom of a boat. Be able to explain how to detect minor faults in starting and running whilst afloat.

2. Complete one of the following two activities:

a. As driver or mechanic member of a power boat's crew:

- Assist in the preparation of the boat for a voyage by checking the engine for possible minor faults, checking the fuel supply and pump, and mustering the fire-fighting equipment.

- In response to orders, operate the engine whilst getting underway from the quay.

- Operate the engine to bring the craft alongside the quay and shut-down.

- Lay out a kedge.

- Re-man the boat in response to a 'distress call' and under orders, start and operate the engine whilst proceeding to and manoeuvring alongside a 'stranded craft'.

- Operate all the boat's gears in a confined area of water and a return journey to base, coming alongside with the tide (or current).

- Know how to leave the engine in a proper manner and how to drain the engine in an emergency.

b. Act as mechanic on at least one short cruise or expedition:

- Be responsible for the running of the engine throughout the cruise.

- Check the engine of a motorboat in preparation for a cruise or expedition to include the provision of fuel and its safe storage, an adequate tool kit and effective fire-fighting apparatus.

- Accompany the expedition either as the mechanic or assistant and be fully or jointly responsible for the operation, care and maintenance of the engine throughout.

Alternative C - aircraft

1. Understand the basic principles of, and be able to point out the component parts of either:

a. an aircraft piston engine; or

b. an aircraft gas turbine engine.

2. Understand the basic principles of flight and airframe construction of a fixed wing aircraft.

3. Know and be able to demonstrate Aircraft Marshalling signals used by day and night.

4. Demonstrate your ability to carry out four of the following:

a. Replenish a light aircraft fuel and oil system.

b. Rig and de-rig a glider.

c. Picket a light aircraft.

d. Change a set of plugs on a light aircraft engine.

e. Inspect aircraft main and tail or nose wheel tyres or serviceability.

f. Repair a small tear in the fabric surface of a light aircraft or glider.

g. The pre-use inspection of a parachute and how to put it on and take it off.

h. Check the control system of a light aircraft or glider for correct sense of movement.

Alternative D – motorcycle or scooter

1. Know the principles of operation of a two-stroke or four-stroke internal combustion engine and understand the function of the clutch, gearbox, carburettor and transmission of a motorcycle.

2. Remove, clean and check the gap of a sparking plug.

3. Check and top up the level of the engine oil.

4. Explain how to adjust the tension of the final drive chain.

5. Show how to change a bulb at the front and in the rear light cluster.

6. Show how to check tyre pressures and inflate a tyre correctly.

7. Remove and replace a road wheel.

8. Explain what to look for when checking that a tyre conforms to the legal requirement.

9. Know the outline requirements for an MOT road test.

→ METEOROLOGIST

Complete the requirements below:

1. Explain how the following are measured:

a. Wind force and direction

b. Cloud type and extent

c. Temperature

d. Pressure

e. Rainfall

f. Humidity

2. Keep a daily record of main weather conditions for at least two weeks.

3. Understand three different ways in which clouds are formed.

4. Know the typical weather produced in your own area by 'warm' and 'cold' air masses in summer and winter, noting the effects of land and sea.

5. Know how synoptic weather maps are produced. Be able to understand a simple map, with fronts and isobars, similar to those shown on television and in newspapers. Relate your observations in requirement 1. to a map.

6. Understand the effects of temperature, wind and water on the human body in cases of hypothermia and exhaustion.

→ MODEL MAKER

Complete the requirements in one of the following alternatives:

Alternative A

1. Construct a model aeroplane, using a kit if desired. When flown, it must meet one of the following target flight performances:

a. Hand launched glider: to fly for 25 seconds

b. Tow-launched glider: to fly for 45 seconds with 50 metres maximum line length

c. Rubber-powered aircraft: to fly for 30 seconds

d. Engine-powered aircraft: to fly for 45 seconds with 15 seconds maximum motor run

e. Control line aircraft: to show a smooth take off and landing, with three laps of level flight at about two metres, with a climb and dive.

2. Discuss the experience of building and flying the model with a knowledgeable adult.

Alternative B

1. Build an electric or engine-powered model boat or yacht not less than 45 cm in length (kits permitted) and show it to be capable of maintaining a straight course of not less than 25 metres.

2. Discuss the experience of building the model with a knowledgeable adult.

Alternative C

1. Choose one of the following two activities:

a. Build an electric slot car racer and drive it a minimum distance of 122 metres on any track without stopping or leaving the slot more than four times.

b. Build a free running car of any type (kits permitted) and demonstrate that it will run for at least 18 metres. Airscrew drive is allowed.

2. Discuss the experience of building the model with a knowledgeable adult.

Alternative D

1. Build a model coach or wagon and demonstrate that it runs satisfactorily behind a scale locomotive.

2. Build a scaled scenic model, such as a station or farmhouse (kits permitted) for a railway layout.

3. Discuss the experience of building your models with a knowledgeable adult.

Alternative E

1. Choose one of the following two activities:

a. Build a model involving the use of a plastic or white metal kit or pre-cast figures.

b. Design and construct a model from wood, plastic or metal construction set (such as Lego or Meccano).

2. Demonstrate knowledge of the different types of kits or parts available in the material you chose.

3. Discuss the experience of building the model with a knowledgeable adult.

→ MY FAITH

Complete the requirements below:

1. Take an active part at your place of worship. This might include getting involved in community work, taking a special part in services or celebrations or following a training or study programme.

2. Find out more about the origins of your faith and share what you found out with others in the Troop.

3. Explore some aspect of the history of your faith at a local, national or international level. This could be done by learning about influential people or by visiting a shrine or other holy place.

4. Be able to explain to an adult some of the teachings of your faith and how these affect the way you live your life.

5. A young person who has been confirmed, had their Bat Mitzvah or Bar Mitzvah or similiar faith life experience will only need to do the following activity to qualify for this badge:

Take part in a Scouting activity relating to their faith.

→ NATURALIST

Complete the requirements below:

Pick one of the following locations and, with appropriate permission, investigate the wildlife and plants found there. This activity should take at least one day.

a. Woodland

b. Parkland

c. Down land

d. Moor land

e. Seashore or sand dune

f. Hedgerow

g. Roadside verge

h. Stream, river or canal

i. Small pond

j. Wetland

k. Marshland

2. Tell a knowledgeable adult what has been discovered using field notes, sketches, photographs or maps prepared on site.

3. Find out more about any one plant, animal or particular wildlife.

4. Discuss what has been found out, giving sources for information, for example museums, field guides or the Internet.

5. Discuss how human activities or management can affect wildlife.

→ BASIC NAUTICAL SKILLS

Complete the requirements below:

1. Swim 50 metres and stay afloat for five minutes.

2. Explain the safety rules that apply to boating, and the effects of winds, tide and current.

3. Demonstrate the difference between a buoyancy aid and a life jacket and explain when each should be used and how they function. Show how they are worn.

4. Complete any two of the following activities:

a. Row a dinghy single-handed and carry out basic manoeuvres.

b. Scull a dinghy and carry out basic manoeuvres.

c. Sail a figure-of-eight course.

d. Complete an introductory course for canoeing or kayaking.

e. Crew a Bell Boat or Dragon Boat.

5. Carry out an activity using knots, bends or hitches. Make a lashing and demonstrate rope whipping or safe sealing.

6. Take part in a half-day expedition or exercise afloat.

7. Complete four items from the list of Nautical Skills Training Activities each one taken from a different section of the list.

8. Keep a log or other record of the water activities completed.

Note: Reference should be made to the Activity Rules in chapter nine of *Policy, Organisation and Rules* and the Adventurous Activity Permit Scheme.

Yellow

→ NAUTICAL SKILLS

Complete the requirements below:

1. Take part in at least two one hour taster sessions in two different water based activities. By the end of the session you will be competent at controlling your craft. This could include, but is not exclusive to:

Canoeing, powered activity, pulling, sailing, wind surfing.

2. Demonstrate that you know how to cope safely if you are involved in a capsize or man overboard situation in the activities used in requirement one.

3. Show how to check water depth (using a method appropriate to your craft), to ensure that you don't ground/beach.

4. Demonstrate that you can tie a figure of eight knot, clove hitch, round turn and two half-hitches, and describe their uses in water activities.

5. Name the parts of one type of craft.

6. Demonstrate and explain what clothing is suitable for the activities used in requirement one.

7. Explain the basic safety rules that apply to the activities undertaken in requirement one.

8. Explain the difference between a buoyancy aid and a life jacket, when each should be used, and how they function. Show how they are worn.

Notes - Reference should be made to the Activity rules in chapter nine of *Policy, Organisation and Rules* and the Adventurous Activity Permit Scheme.

Red

→ ADVANCED NAUTICAL SKILLS

Complete the requirements below:

1. Hold the Nautical Skills Badge.

2. Demonstrate knowledge of pilotage, navigation lights, sound signals, tides, currents and eddies, as relevant to your local waters.

3. Take care of and maintain a boat or canoe for a period of at least three months.

4. Know how to get local weather forecasts, understand their importance and be able to recognise signs of changing weather.

5. Choose two of the following four activities:

a. Gain the RYA Level 2 Power Boat

b. Gain the RYA Start Sailing 3

c. Gain the BCU Paddlepower Discover

d. Gain The Scout Association's Pulling Badge

6. Take part in an expedition afloat lasting at least 24 hours.

7. Obtain a Permit to undertake Water Activities.

8. Complete from the list of Nautical Skills Training Activities:

a. One further item from the practical skills section, making sure that at least two skill areas have been covered.

b. Two further items from the safety section.

c. One further item from the rules of the road and communications section.

d. Three further items from the remaining five sections.

9. Maintain a log or other record of the water activities completed.

Note: Reference should be made to the Activity Rules in chapter nine of *Policy, Organisation and Rules* and the Adventurous Activity Permit Scheme.

→ NAUTICAL SKILLS TRAINING ACTIVITIES

Section 1 - Practical skills

Pulling

1. Gain The Scout Association's Pulling Badge.

2. Gain The Scout Association's Pulling Instructor Badge.

Power

3. Gain The Scout Association Power Coxswain Activity Badge (Narrow boat).

4. Gain the RYA Level 1 Powerboat.

5. Gain the RYA Personal Watercraft Proficiency Award.

Paddle sports

6. Gain the BCU Paddlepower Passport (Kayak/Canadian/Placid Water).

7. Gain the BCU Paddlepower Discover (Kayak/Canadian/Placid Water).

8. Gain the BCU Paddlepower Explore (Kayak/Canadian/Placid Water).

9. Gain the BCU Paddlepower Excel.

10. Gain the Dragon Boating Activity Badge.

Sailing

11. Gain the RYA Youth Windsurfing Level 1.

12. Gain the RYA Youth Windsurfing Level 2.

13. Gain the RYA Youth Windsurfing Level 3.

14. Gain the RYA Young Sailor Scheme Start Sailing 1 Award.

15. Gain the NSSA Bronze Award.

16. Gain the RYA Young Sailor Scheme Start Sailing 2 Award.

17. Gain the NSSA Silver Award.

18. Gain the RYA Young Sailor Scheme Start Sailing 3 Award.

19. Gain the NSSA Gold Award.

20. Gain the RYA Young Sailor Scheme Start Sailing 4 Award.

21. Gain the RYA Young Sailor Scheme Red Badge.

22. Gain the RYA Young Sailor Scheme White Badge.

23. Gain the RYA Young Sailor Scheme Blue Badge.

24. Gain the RYA Competent Crew Certificate.

25. Gain the RYA Sail Cruising Award.

Section 2 - Safety

1. Demonstrate the HELP posture for survival in water.

2. With other Scouts, demonstrate the HUDDLE position for survival in water.

3. Explain how a life jacket works and be able to demonstrate its use.

4. Explain the effects of temperature, wind and water on the human body in cases of hypothermia and exhaustion. List the First Aid procedures in these cases.

5. With another canoeist, demonstrate two methods of canoe rescue.

6. Heave a lifeline from a boat to land within reach of a person eight metres away twice from three attempts.

7. Acting as an assistant in a rescue exercise, board a craft not under control and bring it ashore and single-handed.

8. Under sail, demonstrate the 'man overboard' procedure.

9. Using a training manikin, demonstrate the correct method of artificial ventilation.

10. Demonstrate capsize drill in a sailing dinghy.

11. One other activity of a similar nature and level of achievement as agreed by your leadership team.

Section 3 - Boats and construction

1. Name the parts of a boat or canoe and its equipment. Prepare it for a water activity and use it.

2. With other Scouts, clean, paint or varnish a boat.

3. Under supervision, carry out repairs to a boat or canoe.

4. Demonstrate simple sail repairs, using a palm and needle.

5. Rig a sailing boat and name the parts of the gear.

6. Refit or help build and maintain a boat or canoe.

7. Whilst afloat, construct and hoist a jury rig from available materials in the boat. Sail the jury-rigged boat 500 metres.

8. Under supervision, carry out routine maintenance on an outboard motor. Demonstrate the proper fitting of the motor to the transom of a boat.

9. Make a boat's bag or sail bag.

10. Build and demonstrate a working model of a boat.

11. Lead a team in the safe operation of a lock on a canal

12. One other activity of a similar nature and level of achievement as agreed by your leadership team.

Section 4 - Navigation

1. Read a mariner's compass and have knowledge of variation and deviation.

2. Demonstrate how a position may be found from three bearings.

3. Demonstrate how compass error can be found from a transit bearing.

4. Plot a position using GPS.

5. Demonstrate the use of tide tables and tidal stream atlases.

6. Explain the system of strip maps of canals and rivers. Use such a publication to plan an expedition by canoe or dinghy.

7. Plot your position at sea using Dead Reckoning (DR) and Estimate Position (EP).

8. Using an inland navigation guide, plan a day's cruise in a motor vessel, calculating how long it will take to cover the required distance, taking into account both the number of locks and the mileage involved.

9. Use a sextant to measure vertical angles.

10. Complete a navigation exercise by day on water. Know how to find North by sun or stars.

11. Demonstrate how to take soundings with lead line and pole in local waters.

12. One other activity of a similar nature and level of achievement as agreed by your leadership team.

Section 5 - Rope work and tradition

1. Hoist the colours for a Sea Scout Group. Pipe the 'still' and 'carry on' on a Bosun's call.

2. Demonstrate three further whistle calls commonly used in a Sea Scout Group.

3. Make a sail maker's whipping and one other type of whipping.

4. Make an eye splice and a back splice.

5. Make a short splice.

6. Demonstrate in a nautical setting the following knots with their correct use: clove hitch, rolling hitch, fisherman's bend and a form of stopper knot.

7. With others build a raft from spars and drums and prove it floats.

8. Prepare, coil and throw a heaving line with good accuracy.

9. Make a rope tender or other piece of rope work for example, a lanyard.

10. Explain the differences in usage and stowage of natural and synthetic ropes.

11. One other activity of a similar nature and level of achievement as agreed by your leadership team.

Section 6 - Meteorology

1. Know the Beaufort wind and sea scales.

2. Identify the basic types of clouds. Explain how they are formed, how wind speed is measured and how weather can affect water activities.

3. Record the shipping forecast and explain what it means for any given sea area or inshore waters.

4. Identify the weather associated with frontal systems. Be able to explain the meaning of terms used on a weather map, for example, col, ridge, trough and occlusion.

5. Explain how temperature and pressure are measured.

6. Identify the weather conditions associated with the movement of air masses.

7. Find the geostrophic wind speed from information given on a synoptic chart, and discuss its relationship to wind on land and in coastal waters.

8. Set up a simple weather station and keep a log of daily recordings over a month and make a weather map from it.

9. One other activity of a similar nature and level of achievement as agreed by the leadership team.

Section 7 - Expeditions

1. Demonstrate knowledge of the pulling orders used in single or double-banked boats, and take charge of a pulling boat.

2. Be able to steer and manoeuvre a boat, canoe or dinghy.

3. Complete a one-day expedition with others by canoe, pulling boat or sailing dinghy.

4. Complete a 24 hour expedition with others by water, to include an overnight camp.

5. Form part of a crew on an offshore cruising vessel for not less than 24 hours, to include at least one night afloat.

6. Form part of a crew on an inland cruising vessel for a trip of not less than 48 hours, to include two nights afloat.

7. One other activity of a similar nature and level of achievement as agreed by the leadership team.

Section 8 - Rules of the road and communications

1. Know the rules for getting afloat on tidal waters and on inland waters.

2. Know the International Maritime distress, storm, fog and danger signals.

3. Know the international (IALA. Buoyage System.

4. Know the sound signals used by powered vessels underway and at anchor.

5. Know the navigation lights carried by different types of vessels. Identify at least three different types of vessel from lights displayed.

6. Have a working knowledge of the International Yacht Racing Rules and the Yardstick Handicapping System.

7. Know the effects of currents in non-tidal waterways and the effect of heavy rain in an area drained by a natural river. Explain what is meant by a river in spate and the associated dangers.

8. Advise on suitable moorings and anchorages for different types of craft locally, and give local emergency landing places for small craft.

9. Explain the difficulties of paddling on British waters and how to gain information on access to rivers and lakes. Explain why sensitivity should be shown when launching and landing to other users.

10. Explain the systems of sea-lanes in national and international waters.

11. Gain a VHF licence.

12. One other activity of a similar nature and level of achievement as agreed by the leadership team.

Note: Reference should be made to the Activity Rules in chapter nine of *Policy, Organisation and Rules* and the Adventurous Activity Permit Scheme.

→ **NAVIGATOR**

Complete the requirements in one of the following alternatives:

Alternative A- Land

1. Using 1:50 000 and 1:25 000 scale Ordnance Survey maps complete the following:

a. Show that you understand the meaning of scale, true, grid and magnetic north and can recognise conventional map symbols.

b. Interpret contour lines in terms of shape and steepness of terrain. Know the meaning of topographical features such as valley, col, ridge, spur, etc.

c. Show how to set a map with and without a compass. Be able to use and give six - figure grid references. Demonstrate the use of a romer to improve accuracy.

d. Show how to measure distances on a map and how to estimate timings for a particular route.

e. Show how to find north without the aid of a compass, by day or night.

f. Demonstrate your awareness of the latest developments in electronic technology such as the Global Positioning System.

2. Be familiar with traffic signs and signals as illustrated in The Highway Code.

3. With other Scouts, accompany a motorist on a journey of at least 30 kilometres, taking it in turns to act as navigator to a stated destination. The route should avoid motorways and major roads and if possible should be cross-country, using a variety of roads and lanes. There should be no prior route preparation.

4. Walk two compass routes of at least two kilometres each. One route should have start and end points defined on a map by an adult and the second by the Scout.

5. Demonstrate an ability to:

a. convert grid bearings to magnetic bearings and vice versa

b. use back bearings to check the route

c. estimate current position using a compass

d. walk on a bearing, including 'deviating from course', (the four right angles technique to circumvent an obstacle).

Alternative B - Air

1. Given three headings and corresponding tracks, work out in each case the type and the amount of drift in degrees. Illustrate each case with a simple diagram.

2. Demonstrate with a compass how an aircraft can be turned on to various compass headings.

3. Choose one of the following activities:

a. Draw on a topographical air map a track for an imaginary flight of not less than 80 kilometres. Point out the landmarks that would show up on both sides of the track in clear visibility at an altitude of about 600 metres.

b. Identify on a topographical air map landmarks seen during a flight of about half an hour's duration in clear weather.

4. Illustrate by means of a simple diagram how a fix can be obtained from two position lines. Describe briefly two ways in which bearings can be obtained in an aircraft.

5. Show an understanding of compass headings by completing the following two tasks:

a. Given the true heading and the variation and deviation, work out the compass heading on which the pilot should be flying.

b. Given two sets of true, magnetic and compass headings, work out the variation and deviation in each case.

6. Illustrate latitude and longitude with simple diagrams.

7. Draw on a topographical map the track between any two places not less than 100 kilometres apart and measure the exact distance. Given the aircraft's air speed as 130 km/h, work out the time of flight from overhead starting point to overhead destination in each of the following conditions:

a. With no wind at all

b. With a head wind of 30 km/h

c. With a tail wind of 50 km/h.

8. Demonstrate your awareness of the latest developments in electronic technology such as the Global Positioning System.

Alternative C - Water

1. Have a good working knowledge of charts, chart datum and symbols used.

2. Display an aptitude in compass work by completing the following three activities:

a. Read a mariner's compass marked in points and degrees and have knowledge of compasses generally

b. Know about variation and avoiding deviation. Be able to correct a magnetic compass course for variation and deviation to obtain a true bearing. Given a true bearing, successfully adjust this to obtain a compass course

c. Understand how compass error can be found from a transit bearing.

3. Complete two of the following:

a. Understand how a position may be found from two intersecting position lines

b. Understand what is meant by a 'cocked hat' position and how to use it safely. Plot a position from any three cross bearings

c. Plot a position using the 'running fix' method

d. Plot a position using a combination of compass bearings and any one or more of the following:

- Satellite navigation system

- vertical sextant angle

- horizontal sextant angle

- line of soundings

- transits

4. Be able to use tide tables and tidal stream atlases.

5. Understand the use of the marine log to obtain distance run and speed.

6. Understand the buoyage system for United Kingdom coastal waters and other methods of marking dangers and channels.

7. Demonstrate your awareness of the latest developments in electronic technology such as the Global Positioning System and electronic charts.

8. Undertake a coastal voyage of between four and six hours acting as navigator. A log should be kept showing courses steered, distance run, navigation marks passed and weather experienced. During the voyage:

- plot the estimated position every hour by keeping up the dead reckoning

- whenever appropriate, and not less than once per hour, plot an observed position by bearings or other means of obtaining a fix

Note: The voyage should be planned on the chart beforehand using tidal streams to the best advantage and giving hourly courses to steer for an assumed speed.

Alternative D - Introductory GPS navigation

1. Demonstrate an awareness of the Global Positioning System (GPS) to include:

a. How it works

b. Ownership and control of the system

c. Benefits and society

d. What factors affect accuracy

2. Programme a hand-held GPS receiver to perform the following functions:

a. Find your location (grid reference and latitude/longitude) and record it

b. Enter the grid reference of a local landmark and navigate to the waypoint

c. Enter the latitude/longitude coordinates of a nearby point and navigate to the waypoint, checking the accuracy

d. Walk on a bearing using the GPS and a map

3. Demonstrate an understanding of the differences between Ordnance Survey and latitude/longitude coordinates.

4. Using an Ordnance Survey May (1:25 000 or 1:50 00 scale) plan a route of at least 4KM that contains a minimum of 10 waypoints. Discuss the features and challenges that exist along the route. Programme the route into a hand-held GPS and undertake the journey.

5. Sign up to a geocaching website. Find out about geocaching and demonstrate an understanding of what is involved in both locating and placing a geocache.

6. Demonstrate an understanding of the safety and environmental aspects of geocaching, e.g. relevant Activity Rules in chapter nine of Policy, Organisation and Rules; Highway Code; Countryside Code and guidelines produced by the Geocaching Association of Great Britain (GAGB).

7. Find five geocaches using a GPS, at least 3 of which must be 'multi-caches' with at least two waypoints. Discuss the accuracy of the information provided and of the GPS receiver you used.

8. With adult assistance where necessary:

a. Plan, assemble and hide 2 caches, one of which should be a multi-cache. The planning should involve making sure the location is suitable and that other navigators have proper access to the land and terrain

b. Either submit your caches to a geocaching website, or give the details to other Scouts to successfully find the caches

Note: Reference should be made to the Activity Rules in chapter nine of Policy, Organisation and Rules and the Adventurous Activity Permit Scheme.

→ ORIENTEER

Complete the requirements below:

1. Know the map colours and common symbols used on an orienteering map.

2. Be able to orientate a map using either terrain or compass and understand how to navigate whilst keeping the map set to the ground. Be able to 'thumb' the map to log a changing position.

3. Complete three courses at orienteering events recognised by the BOF, or of other similar standard.

4. Show knowledge of safety procedures, basic First Aid, appropriate clothing and equipment for countryside navigation.

5. Demonstrate knowledge of the Countryside Code.

Note: A Scout who has qualified for the Yellow Standard Award of the British Orienteering Federation automatically qualifies for this badge.

→ PADDLE SPORTS

Complete the requirements below:

1. Complete the British Canoe Union's Paddlepower Passport levels 2-5.

Note: Reference should be made to the Activity Rules in chapter nine of *Policy, Organisation and Rules* and the Adventurous Activity Permit Scheme.
More details at www.bcu.org.uk

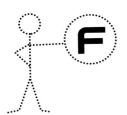

→ PARASCENDING

Complete the requirements below:

1. Know the rules relating to Access to Airfields as laid down in *Policy, Organisation and Rules* and The Scout Association factsheet on parascending.

2. Take part in a parascending course and be able to:

a. demonstrate a good landing roll

b. be able to put on a harness and adjust it

c. assist on more than two occasions as tensiometer reader, observer or log keeper.

3. Know the main characteristics and different types of parachutes used by parascenders.

4. Show a basic knowledge of the theory of flight.

5. Experience at least four parascending flights. (Where a Scout is under 14 years, flights must be taken in tandem, and under the instruction of a BHPA dual qualified instructor).

Note: Reference should be made to the Activity Rules in chapter nine of *Policy, Organisation and Rules* and the Adventurous Activity Permit Scheme.

→ PHOTOGRAPHER

Complete the requirements in one of the following alternatives:

Alternative A - Still photography

1. Choose one of these two activities:

a. Produce 12 prints of photographs (negative or digital. taken by yourself covering at least two different aspects from this list:

– portrait

– still life or similar

– land or seascape

– sport or similar action

– flash-gun

– time-lapse photography.

b. Produce six black and white photographs where you have undertaken some part of the processing.

2. Choose one from the following two activities:

a. Show knowledge of the main functions of a film camera, including shutter speed, aperture, film speed, depth of field and lens focusing.

b. Show knowledge of the main functions of a digital camera including resolution, digital compression and how these affect the final print. Show knowledge of the types of removable memory available.

3. Discuss the different types of camera and the accessories available.

4. Choose one from the following activities:

a. Describe the process of developing black and white films and prints, including the use of an enlarger.

b. Describe the processes and equipment needed to produce prints from a digital camera, including the use of editing software.

c. Describe the processes and equipment needed to scan prints or negatives from existing photographs, including the use of editing software.

5. Diagnose faults that occur both at the photographing or printing stages, such as over/under exposure and high/low contrast. Explain the difference between camera shake and subject movement.

6. Demonstrate that you know how to care for a camera and accessories.

Alternative B - Video photography

1. Produce at least two short films from two of the following categories:

a. documentary

b. music video

c. drama

d. situation comedy

e. advertisement

f. training film

g. environmental

h. community

i. current affairs.

A story board and script should be produced for each of these. The film can be edited 'in camera' or by using simple editing equipment.

2. Discuss the following:

a. The main features and functions of a video camera, including zoom, focus, aperture, shutter speed, white balance and common tape formats.

b. Problems that may be encountered when using automatic settings and how these may be overcome.

3. Show an understanding of the following:

a. Camera techniques such as panning, zooming, the use of close-ups, long shots, and the use of additional lighting.

b. Production techniques such as editing, how to avoid jumpy cuts, maintaining continuity.

4. Demonstrate that you know how to care for a video camera and accessories such as tapes, batteries, microphones and lights.

Note: Alternative B requirements 1 can be completed as a small group with each person taking a different responsibility, for example camera operator, director, or editor.

→ PHYSICAL RECREATION

Complete the requirements below:

1. Take a regular part in an active sport or physical pursuit for which an Activity Badge has not been gained. This can be a team game such as rugby, football, cricket or water polo; or an individual sport such as tennis, squash, running or gymnastics; or a pursuit such as walking, yoga, ice skating, dancing or keep fit.

2. Be able to demonstrate a reasonable level of skill in the sport or pursuit and give evidence of improvement.

3. Explain the rules or guidelines that govern the sport or pursuit chosen.

4. Demonstrate the preparations they make before taking part in the sport or pursuit. These may include any special equipment or clothes required and/or warm-up and warm-down routines.

Notes: This badge is for those who regularly take part in sport or physical pursuit activities for which there is no specific Activity Badge. A Scout can gain more than one Physical Recreation Badge for different sports or pursuits.

The sport or pursuit chosen should not be that which forms part of the school curriculum. It may, however, include school sports played after school or at weekends.

→ PIONEER

Complete the requirements below:

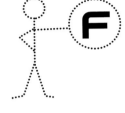

1. As a member of a group, take part in the following:

a. An indoor pioneering project, for example, constructing a guided missile launcher or chariot

b. An outdoor pioneering project, for example, building a monkey bridge, a raft, a parallel or aerial runway.

2. Demonstrate the following:

a. A whipping or safe rope sealing

b. A splice

c. The correct way to coil and store a rope

d. The use of simple blocks and tackle

e. The use of levers to extract objects or move heavy weights

f. Anchorages for firm and soft ground

g. An understanding of the need for supervision and safety in pioneering projects.

3. Name and tie at least six knots and three lashings useful in pioneering.

Note: Reference should be made to the Aerial Runway Code (FS120004) and the Activity Rules in chapter nine of *Policy, Organisation and Rules.*

→ POWER COXSWAIN

Complete all the requirements in one of the following alternatives.

Alternative A – Powerboats

1. Qualify for the RYA Level 1 Powerboat Award.

2. Carry out a Scout activity as a coxswain of a powered craft (plaining or displacement), demonstrating safe procedures and courtesy to other water users.

Alternative B – Narrow boats

1. Have a general knowledge of the canal system and, using a navigation guide, identify the following:

a. Suitable places to moor and wind

b. Locks, bridges and local hazards

c. Location of water points and sanitary stations

d. Location of shops and telephone.

2. Using a navigation guide, calculate how long it will take to cover a given distance, taking into account both the number of locks and the mileage involved.

3. Know the safety precautions necessary with regard to:

a. fire-fighting appliances

b. man overboard drill.

c. locks

d. tunnels.

4. Show knowledge of the principles of a marine engine by:

a. starting and stopping an engine, changing gear and know the effect of transverse thrust with a single screw

b. recognising fouling of the screw due to weed or rubbish and knowing how to clear it with engine stopped

c. using the stern grease gland screw.

5. Prepare the boat for service and, with the help of a crew, cast off and leave moorings.

6. Show an ability to control the boat by:

a. steering past moored boats

b. steering past a boat travelling in the opposite direction.

c. steering through a bridge.

d. bringing the boat alongside a bank and mooring up.

e. turning in a winding hole and manoeuvring in confined water, such as a marina.

f. taking the boat through a lock with the help of a crew.

g. Stopping the boat quickly using reverse gear. Be aware of the dangers of anything in the water behind the boat.

Note: Reference should be made to the Activity Rules in chapter nine of *Policy, Organisation and Rules* and the Adventurous Activity Permit Scheme.

→ **PUBLIC RELATIONS**

Complete the requirements below:

1. Complete one of the following:

a. Produce and use a presentation about Scouting using audio and visual media, which can be shown to other people not involved in Scouting.

b. Produce and use a presentation about your Troop using a mixture of audio and visual media that can be shown to a Beaver Colony, Cub Pack or parents in your Group.

2. Find out about local media outlets (for example: radio, TV, newspapers and online opportunities). Make contact with your local Media Development Manager to consider coverage of a positive news story or feature connected with local Scouting.

3. Complete two of the following:

a. Prepare and present a live report (either to camera or microphone) at a Scouting event or activity. The report should be accurate and informative and reflect the adventure of Scouting.

b. Prepare a static display about your Troop or Group that can be exhibited in your local library, Information Centre, or other similar public place.

c. Help to design a website for your Group or Troop and maintain it for at least two months.

d. Interview a local personality, public figure or someone in the local news (e.g. Church leader, politician, media celebrity). Present the interview to your Troop. Take advice from a Leader before contacting the person.

e. Write a report about a local Scout activity and get it published in one or more of the following:

– Your Group, District or County newsletter or website

– *Scouting* magazine or on the scouts.org.uk/scouts website

– The local press.

→ **PULLING**

Complete the requirements below:

1. Row a dinghy single-handed and carry out in sequence the following manoeuvres:

a. Take the boat away from a bank side mooring.

b. Row in a straight line for 100 metres.

c. Complete a figure-of-eight course.

d. Scull over the stern between two points 20 metres apart and turn through 180 degrees.

e. Draw stroke over the bow.

2. Using a round turn and two half hitches, moor to a ring, post or bollard.

3. Be able to point out and name the basic parts of a pulling boat.

4. As part of the crew of a boat complete the following:

a. Take a place as an oarsman, including stroke.

b. Understand boat orders and be able to act on them.

c. As bowman, be a lookout and report hazards to the coxswain using standard maritime directions e.g. starboard, port quarter, dead ahead, etc.

5. From a boat, heave an unweighted line to land within reach of target five metres away with not more than three attempts.

6. Understand the safety rules that apply to Scout boating.

7. Know the difference between a lifejacket and a buoyancy aid and show the correct method of wear.

8. Understand the importance of wearing appropriate clothing for various weather conditions.

9. Know what actions and safety requirements to take when being towed.

10. Have a basic knowledge of 'Rules of the Road' for your local waters.

Note: Reference should be made to the Activity Rules in chapter nine of *Policy, Organisation and Rules* and the Adventurous Activity Permit Scheme.

→ **QUARTERMASTER**

Complete the requirements in one of the following alternatives:

Alternative A

1. Assist a Group or Troop Quartermaster for an agreed period to show ability in the following areas:

a. Care and storage of tentage, including how to do simple repairs

b. Care and storage of cordage, to include whipping, splicing, hanking, coiling and safety inspections

c. Safe storage and handling of fuels used by the Troop or Group such as methylated spirits, paraffin, petrol and gas

d. Care of cooking stoves and cooking utensils, to include simple repairs, cleaning and general maintenance

e. Convenient storage of the Troop or Group's training and games equipment

f. Care and storage of equipment used for adventurous activities. For example, sailing gear, canoes and paddles, lifejackets and buoyancy aids, go-karts, or climbing ropes.

2. Be able to keep a simple record showing equipment issued and returned.

3. Understand that general tidiness is the secret of good quartermastering. Explain how this is achieved in the Troop or Group store.

Alternative B

1. As Equipment Quartermaster, assist at a Nights Away experience for at least two days. During this time show ability in at least three of the following areas:

a. Care and maintenance of all tentage, including the ability to do simple repairs to guy lines and fabric tears

b. Care and storage of all cordage, to include whipping, splicing, hanking, coiling and safety inspections

c. Safe storage and handling of fuels used by the camp, such as methylated spirits, paraffin, petrol and gas

d. Care, maintenance and general storage of all tools such as axes, spades and saws

e. Care and storage of equipment used for adventurous activities such as sailing gear, canoes and paddles, lifejackets and buoyancy aids, and climbing ropes.

2. Be able to keep simple records showing equipment issued and returned.

3. Maintain and replenish a portable First Aid kit.

4. Select tools to take to camp to complete emergency repairs on equipment

5. Understand that general tidiness is the secret of good quartermastering. Explain how this was achieved at the Nights Away experience at which the Quartermaster assisted.

Alternative C

1. Assist at a residential experience for at least two days, by taking on the role of Food Quartermaster. Complete the following:

a. Plan a balanced menu for the event.

b. Draw up a complete shopping list

c. Assist in the purchasing of food and account for the money spent.

d. Help arrange the transport of food to the venue.

e. Supervise the safe storing of food. Explain how to keep fresh food cool in a camping environment, without refrigeration, how to protect from rodents, vermin and insects and how to avoid cross contamination of foods.

f. Demonstrate the importance of cleanliness and good hygiene when allocating food ensuring that the right items and quantities are issued for each meal.

g. Supervise the disposal of waste and unused food.

h. Look after and maintain any cooking stoves and other cooking utensils.

2. Understand that general tidiness is the secret of good quartermastering. Explain how this was achieved at the Nights Away experience at which the Quartermaster assisted.

→ SMALLHOLDER

Complete the requirements in one of the following alternatives:

Alternative A

1. Have a good knowledge of farming practices in your locality.

2. Know the organisation and daily and seasonal operations of a farm of your own choice, with special reference to the livestock, crops, cultivation, rotation, machinery and labour force.

3. Discuss the changes in farming practices that have taken place recently in your locality and the reasons for these.

Alternative B

1. Cultivate an area of garden or an allotment for a period agreed beforehand with your leadership team.

2. Grow successfully three kinds of hardy annual flower, three kinds of vegetable and two kinds each of bulbs, herbaceous plants and flowering shrubs or roses. As an alternative, grow eight types of plant.

3. Discuss the work done and the results achieved.

Alternative C

1. Keep any kind of livestock for a period agreed beforehand with the leadership team. For example:

   - For farm animals or birds, know how they should be housed, fed, bred and their economic uses. Show how to handle them safely and know about animal welfare

   - Manage a hive. Show some of the honey produced.

Note: An experienced adult adviser will be required to oversee the activities.

→ SNOWSPORTS

Complete the requirements below:

1. Demonstrate knowledge of the following:

a. The clothing and protective equipment to wear for different weather conditions, snow and artificial surfaces

b. The safety features of your equipment (bindings, brakes etc.).

c. The importance of warming-up before taking part in snowsports

d. The importance of drinking plenty of fluids especially in the mountain environment

e. The safest places to stop on a run

f. The importance of staying together as a group

g. What to do in the event of an accident

h. The FIS safety code (published by the *Federation International de Ski).*

i. The hazards of the mountain environment for snowsports.

2. Complete one of the following:

a. Qualify for Snowlife Snowsport Ski Award level 2.

b. Qualify for Snowlife Snowsport Snowboard Award level 2.

c. Qualify for Snowsport England Nordic Award level 1.

d. Complete at least 16 hours of Snowsports as part of a family or education holiday to a ski resort.

Notes: In France, an equivalent level would be the 'ESF Flocon [which means 'snowflake'] or One Star' and in Italy the Scuola Italiana di Sci One and Two Star Bronze.

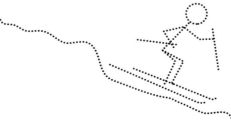

→ SPORTS ENTHUSIAST

Complete the requirements below:

Demonstrate your interest in a sport that you follow by completing the requirements below:

1. Explain the rules governing the chosen sport.

2. Describe the levels of achievement within the sport either locally or, nationally or internationally.

3. Show knowledge of some of the personalities, champions or other experts within the sport and explain how they might have inspired you.

4. Talk about the equipment required for the sport.

5. Describe a recent major event, championship or landmark in the sport.

6. Explain how you follow the sport and how you keep up to date with developments.

Note: The Badge is designed for those who follow a sport, rather than participate. While many Scouts might choose football or basketball, the requirements could encompass sports as diverse as archery, motor racing and water polo. Scouts may gain more than one Sports Enthusiast Badge.

→ STREET SPORTS

Complete the requirements below:

1. Take a regular part in a street sport such as skateboarding, BMXing, roller or in-line skating or another street sport as agreed with the leadership team.

2. Complete the activities below:

a. Own or use equipment for a street sport for six months. Be able to check, adjust and repair the equipment to ensure safe use.

b. Be able to demonstrate a reasonable level of skill in the chosen street sport and show evidence of improvement.

3. Explain the safety rules for your chosen sport.

4. Demonstrate ability in the chosen sport to other people or your Troop. This could be an exhibition or a public event or competition.

→ SURVIVAL SKILLS

Complete the requirements below:

1. Demonstrate knowledge of the following:

a. How to prevent and treat the effects of extreme heat (sunstroke and dehydration) and cold (hypothermia)

b. The First Aid treatment for external bleeding and shock, the correct method of applying mouth-to-mouth breathing and the dangers involved in moving injured people

c. How to construct different kinds of shelter

d. How to build several different types of fire and the burning qualities of different woods

e. The correct use of International Distress Signals, using whistle, torch, mirror or markers

f. Some basic actions to take while awaiting rescue that will both keep you (and your group) safe and will assist your rescuers in locating you

g. Some edible plants and/or fruit to be found locally

h. Methods of filtering and purifying water.

2. With a group of at least three Scouts, take part in a survival exercise lasting about 24 hours, during which the group should complete the following:

a. Construct a shelter of natural or salvaged materials and sleep in it.

b. Cook all meals over an open fire.

c. Cook without utensils or aluminium foil. A knife may be used.

d. Demonstrate methods of finding direction by day or night without a compass.

Notes: Requirement 1 must be completed before requirement 2 is undertaken. The leadership team should select suitable country for this so that supervision is possible. Wild mountainous country is not intended. The Nights Away Scheme must be followed. Alternative activities may be undertaken as agreed with the leadership team.

→ WATER SPORTS

Complete one of the following requirements:

Badges and Awards

Participation Awards

Chief Scout's Gold Award

Challenge Badges

⁚› Activity Badges

   Sports Enthusiast

   Street Sports

   Survival Skills

   Water Sports

   World Faiths

Staged Activity Badges

Activity Plus Badges

Instructor Badges

Partnership Awards

1. Qualify for the British Rowing Learn to Row Passport – Stage 1.

2. Qualify for the Snorkel Diver Award of the British Sub-aqua Club.

3. Qualify for the British Surfing Association's Junior Scheme Level 3 Award.

4. Qualify for the British Water Ski & Wakeboard – Cutting Edge Bronze Award.

5. Qualify for the Royal Yachting Association National Windsurfing Scheme Level 1.

6. Qualify for the Discover Scuba Diving Award of the Professional Association of Diving Instructors

Reference should be made to the Activity Rules in chapter nine of *Policy, Organisation and Rules* and the Adventurous Activity Permit Scheme.

→ WORLD FAITHS

Complete the requirements below:

1. Complete one of the following activities:

a. Visit a place of worship for a faith other than your own and find out the differences between this building and your own place of worship. Examples include Gurdwara, temple, Mosque, Church or Synagogue.

b. Attend a religious festival from a faith different to your own.

2. Complete one of the following activities:

a. Learn about the life of a founder or a prominent leader of a Faith other than your own (such as Prince Siddartha Gautama, Mohammed, Jesus Christ, Mahatma Gandhi or a saint such as St George)

b. Find out about someone from another faith, whose faith has had a significant impact upon his or her life.

3. Read a sacred text from another faith and show how it compares it with a similar teaching from your own faith.

4. Find out how following the teachings of another faith affects an individual's daily life. This could include food or dietary laws, rituals, prayers or religious observances.

Discuss your findings with others in the Troop.

→ WRITER

Complete any four requirements from those below, discussing the choice with an appropriate adult:

1. Compose a poem of at least eight lines and discuss its meaning and construction.

2. Write a short story of around 600 words around an idea agreed with an appropriate adult beforehand.

3. Write a descriptive passage of around 600 words on a subject agreed with an appropriate adult beforehand.

4. Write a 400-word review of a favourite book, play or other work of literature and discuss this with an appropriate adult.

5. Produce a published article of around 500 words in length. This could be in the form of a contribution to a school, faith community or Scout magazine or a letter to a local paper.

6. Keep a diary on a subject and for a length of time agreed with an appropriate adult beforehand.

7. Write a play or dramatic sketch lasting at least 10 minutes.

8. Interview a local celebrity, or other interesting person. Write or type out the interview to show the questions you asked and the interviewee's replies.

9. Write a letter to a pen pal (real or imaginary) of at least 150 words.

10. Read a piece of your work in front of an audience.

→ STAGED ACTIVITY BADGES

→ EMERGENCY AID STAGES 1-5

Complete the following:

Emergency Aid Notes:

Young people should be trained and assessed using the syllabus and resources provided in conjunction with the British Red Cross. These are published on www.scouts.org.uk/emergencyaid and supporting programme material for the first three stages can be found on Programmes Online. At each stage Leaders should not assume prior knowledge but should cover the full syllabus using instruction games and exercises to reinforce the learning.
For stages 1 - 3 ongoing assessment is acceptable. For stages 4 and 5 a more structured assessment at the end of the course is recommended to test knowledge.

→ EMERGENCY AID - STAGE 1

Complete the requirements below:

1. Understand and recognise dangers in the house and outside.

2. Know what to do at the scene of an accident.

3. Know how to open an airway.

4. Know how to treat minor cuts, scratches and grazes.

Note: This stage requires *one to two hours* activity/learning and should be trained and assessed by an adult or Young Leader familiar with the resource material.

→ EMERGENCY AID – STAGE 2

Complete the requirements below:

1. Know what to do at the scene of an accident.
2. Know how to get help from the emergency services.
3. Know how to clear an airway, give rescue breaths and place in the recovery position.
4. Know how to deal with minor bleeding.
5. Know how to deal with major bleeding.
6. Know how to deal with burns and scalds.

Note: This requires *two to three hours* of training/activity and should be trained and assessed by an adult or Young Leader with First Response or equivalent external qualifications and who is familiar with the resource material.

A young person holding first aid award covering this or a similar syllabus from a recognised First Aid provider (for example St John's Ambulance or the British Red Cross) automatically qualifies for this award.

→ EMERGENCY AID – STAGE 3

Complete the requirements below:

1. Know what to do at the scene of an accident.
2. Know when and how to contact the emergency services.
3. Be able to respond to the needs of an unconscious patient. Know how to open an airway, give CPR and how to place in the recovery position.
4. Know how to deal with major bleeding.
5. Know how to deal with burns and scalds.
6. Know how to safeguard against the effects of heat. Know how to recognise and treat heat exhaustion.
7. Know how to safeguard against the effects of cold. Know how to recognise and treat hypothermia.
8. Recognise the symptoms of shock and how to treat a casualty.
9. Know how to deal with choking.

Note: This stage requires *four to five hours* of training and activity and should be trained and assessed by an adult with current experience of First Aid training, who holds a First Response or equivalent external qualification and is familiar with the resource material.

A young person holding first aid award covering this or a similar syllabus from a recognised First Aid provider (for example St John's Ambulance or the British Red Cross) automatically qualifies for this award.

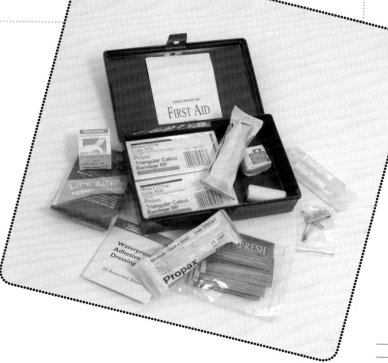

→ EMERGENCY AID – STAGE 4

Complete the requirements below:

1. Know what to do at the scene of an accident.

2. Know when and how to contact the emergency services.

3. Be able to respond to the needs of an unconscious patient. Know how to open an airway, give CPR to both an adult and a child and how to place in the recovery position.

4. Know how to deal with both minor cuts and bleeding and major bleeding injuries.

5. Know how to deal with burns and scalds.

6. Know how to safeguard against the effects of heat. Know how to recognise and treat heat exhaustion.

7. Know how to safeguard against the effects of cold. Know how to recognise and treat hypothermia.

8. Recognise the symptoms of shock and how to treat a casualty.

9. Know how to deal with choking.

10. Know the common medication procedures used by individuals with asthma and how to deal with an asthma attack.

11. Know how to recognise the symptoms of a heart attack and take appropriate action.

12. Know how to deal with an injury to the head.

13. Know how to deal with a casualty with a suspected spinal injury.

14. Recognise the signs of a fracture and soft tissue injuries and how to protect from further injury or pain.

15. Know the signs and symptoms of Meningitis and the action to take.

Note: This stage requires *eight hours* of training and activity and should be trained and assessed by arrangement with an adult holding a full First Aid qualification and validated skills from the Adult Training Scheme in Presenting and Facilitating. Alternatively, a qualified First Aid Trainer from an externally recognised organisation may fulfil this role.

A young person holding first aid award covering this or a similar syllabus from a recognised First Aid provider (for example St John's Ambulance or the British Red Cross) automatically qualifies for this award.

This award exceeds the requirements of First Response and is a suitable alternative to the Young Leaders' Module K First Aid Master Class.

→ EMERGENCY AID – STAGE 5

Complete the requirements below:

1. Know what to do at the scene of an accident.

2. Know when and how to contact the emergency services.

3. Be able to respond to the needs of an unconscious patient. Know how to open an airway, give CPR to adults, children and infants and how to place in the recovery position.

4. Know how to deal with both minor cuts and bleeding and major bleeding injuries.

5. Know how to deal with burns and scalds.

6. Know how to safeguard against the effects of heat. Know how to recognise and treat heat exhaustion.

7. Know how to safeguard against the effects of cold. Know how to recognise and treat hypothermia.

8. Recognise the symptoms of shock and how to treat a casualty.

9. Know how to deal with choking.

10. Know the common medication procedures used by asthmatics and how to deal with an asthma attack.

11. Know how to recognise the symptoms of a heart attack and take appropriate action.

12. Know how to deal with an injury to the head. Know how to treat a casualty with a suspected spinal injury.

13. Recognise the signs of a fracture and how to protect from further injury or pain.

14. Know how to recognise the symptoms of a stroke and take appropriate action.

15. Know how to recognise a range of muscular and skeletal injuries and how to protect from further injury and pain.

16. Know how to recognise and deal with a range of other medical conditions including Anaphylaxis, Angina, Cramp, Diabetes, Epilepsy, Febrile Convulsions and Meningitis.

Note: This stage requires 16 hours of training and activity and should be trained and assessed by a holder of a current externally recognised First Aid Trainer qualification.

A young person holding first aid award covering this or a similar syllabus from a recognised First Aid provider (for example St John's Ambulance or the British Red Cross) automatically qualifies for this award.

→ **HIKES AWAY**

Complete the requirements below:

Hikes Away 1

Complete one hike or journey with a purpose as agreed with the Leader. Those taking part should be dressed and equipped for the prevailing conditions and terrain.

Hikes Away 5

Complete five hikes or journeys with a purpose as agreed with the Leader. Those taking part should be dressed and equipped for the prevailing conditions and terrain.

Hikes Away 10

Complete 10 hikes or journeys with a purpose as agreed with the Leader. Those taking part should be dressed and equipped for the prevailing conditions and terrain.

Hikes Away 20

Complete 20 hikes or journeys with a purpose as agreed with the Leader. Those taking part should be dressed and equipped for the prevailing conditions and terrain.

Hikes Away 35

Complete 35 hikes or journeys with a purpose as agreed with the Leader. Those taking part should be dressed and equipped for the prevailing conditions and terrain

Hikes Away 50

Complete 50 hikes or journeys with a purpose as agreed with the Leader. Those taking part should be dressed and equipped for the prevailing conditions and terrain.

Notes: Reference should be made to the Activity Rules in Chapter 9 of *Policy, Organisation and Rules* and the Activity Permit Scheme.

Examples of activities qualifying for a 'Hike Away' are listed below. Other similar activities could be undertaken.

For the Scout Section

Plan for at least four hours of activities. Examples might be:

- Take part in a dusk to dawn hike.

- Explore a bridleway on horseback.

- An overnight expedition by foot (which would count as two hikes).

- A trip down a river in an open canoe.

- Complete a 20km cycle ride as part of the Cyclist Activity Badge.

→ INFORMATION TECHNOLOGY – STAGES 1–5

Complete the requirements below:

INFORMATION TECHNOLOGY – STAGE 1

Complete the following:

1. Show that you can switch on and close down a computer safely.

2. Show that you know what the following are:

- monitor
- mouse
- printer
- DVD Drive
- Icon
- Web cam
- Microphone
- USB Drive

3. Use a piece of software of your choice to show that you can produce a poster to show others what you do in Scouting. It should include both text and graphics.

4. Use a piece of painting software of your choice to produce a simple picture.

5. Show that you can use a piece of software that requires the use of a CD-ROM.

INFORMATION TECHNOLOGY – STAGE 2

Complete the following:

1. Produce a list of rules for using the internet safely and what dangers can be found on the Internet (Link to CEOP guidance)

2. Describe what you would use each of the items listed in Stage 1:

3. Show that you can save a file and open that file at a later date.

4. Choose two additional activities out of:

a. Access the internet safely, to research a topic of your choice and create a short presentation using the software of your choice

b. Use a digital camera to take some digital photographs and use a piece of software to enhance or alter the original photographs.

c. Use a piece of software of your choice to produce a set of matching stationery for an event, eg birthday, place cards, invitations, posters etc.

d. Produce a series of newsletters for your section over a three-month period.

INFORMATION TECHNOLOGY – STAGE 3

Complete the following:

1. Show knowledge about the history of the Internet and how it works. Suggest how you think it may be used in the future.

2. Describe the advantages of using IT compared to manual systems in two of the following:

- Banking
- Keeping in touch with friends
- Shopping
- Keeping up with the news and weather
- Research

3. Using email, demonstrate that you can:

- send an email
- reply to a sender
- reply to more than one sender
- open an attachment

4. Explain what computer virus, malware and spyware are, the possible effects and how they can be prevented.

5. Choose three additional activities out of the following:

a. Use a piece of presentation software (eg Powerpoint) to give a presentation of your choice to an audience.

b. Devise a simple database that could be used by your section for a particular purpose, eg camp records, general records.

c. Produce a local map showing local facilities and places of interest.

d. Describe the environmental impact of a PC

e. Produce a storyboard for a game idea you might have, include any key features and describe how the game is completed/won.

INFORMATION TECHNOLOGY – STAGE 4

Complete the following:

1. Explain to the assessor the laws which concern the copying of software, access to computer systems and storage of personal information.

2. Create a simple website for your section.

3. Explain how an IT system is used by a major user, eg a supermarket chain or a bank.

4. Show how that you have used IT in your daily life over the last six months, eg to research, download music etc.

5. Explain the following terminology:

- macros
- web publishing
- video conferencing
- multi-tasking
- drag and drop.

6. Choose two additional activities out of the following:

a. Evaluate a range of professional websites.

b. Produce a range of information literature on an agreed theme, eg 'how to be more environmentally friendly' - leaflets, posters, fliers etc.

c. Produce a complex database for a specific purpose.

d. Take part in a video conference with a Scout from another part of the world. (An idea opportunity would be Jamboree on The Internet which happens every October).

e. Demonstrate your ability to use a control programme, eg Lego Dacta, LOGO beyond a basic standard.

f. Create a list of social networking sites, list what you use them for and how you use them and the Internet safely.

INFORMATION TECHNOLOGY – STAGE 5

Complete the following:

1. Design an integrated system using a number of pieces of software that, for example, a small company would need, such as a database, letters, invoices etc.

2. Design a website that has a series of pages and which includes links to other sites of a similar nature.

3. Reflect critically on the impact of IT on your own life and that of others - consider political, social, ethical, economic, moral and legal issues.

4. Produce an 'internet guide' for children of a younger age.

5. Produce a list of websites that would interest other Members of The Scout Association in the same section as you.

→ MUSICIAN STAGES 1-5

Complete the requirements below:

MUSICIAN - STAGE 1

Complete the following:

Skill

1. Listen to a short tune of a couple of lines and then sing it back.

2. Listen to another tune and then beat or clap out the rhythm.

Performance

3. Sing or play two different types of song or tune on your chosen instrument.

   This performance must be either in front of other Scouts, or at a public performance, such as a Group Show, school concert or church service.

Knowledge

4. Demonstrate some of the musical exercises that you use to practice your skills.

5. Talk about your instrument, and why you enjoy playing it (or the songs you sing and why you enjoy singing them).

6. Name several well-known pieces of music that can be played on your instrument.

7. Name several musicians who you have heard.

Interest

8. Tell your assessor about the music you most like to listen to.

MUSICIAN - STAGE 2

Complete the following:

Skill

1. Achieve Grade One of the Associated Board of the Royal School of Music (or similar) on the instrument of your choice.

Performance

2. Sing or play two different types of song or tune on your chosen instrument. This performance must be either in front of other Scouts, or at a public performance, such as a Group Show, school concert or church service.

Knowledge:

3. Demonstrate some of the musical exercises that you use to practice your skills.

4. Talk about your instrument and why you enjoy playing it (or the songs you sing and why you enjoy singing them).

5. Name several well-known pieces of music associated with your instrument.

6. Name several musicians who are associated with your instrument or chosen songs.

Interest

7. Talk about your own interests in music, including what you listen to most, and how this is similar to or different from the music you play or sing.

MUSICIAN – STAGE 3

Complete the following:

Skill

1. Achieve Grade Two of the Associated Board of the Royal School of Music (or similar) on the instrument of your choice.

Performance

2. Sing or play (either as a solo or with others) two different types of song or tune on your chosen instrument. This performance must be either in front of the other Scouts, or at a public performance such as a Group Show, school concert or church service

Knowledge

3. Demonstrate some of the musical exercises that you use to practice your skills.

4. Talk about your instrument and why you enjoy playing it (or the songs you sing and why you enjoy singing them).

5. Talk about several well-known pieces of music associated with your instrument or chosen songs.

Interest

6. Talk about your own interests in music, including what you listen to most, and how this is similar to or different from the music you play or sing.

MUSICIAN – STAGE 4

Complete the following:

Skill

1. Achieve Grade Three or Four of the Associated Board of the Royal School of Music (or similar) on the instrument of your choice.

Performance

2. Sing or play three different types of song or tune on your chosen instrument. One should be a solo and one of the other two should accompany other musicians in an arrangement of their choice. The performance should be public, such as at a Group Show, school concert or church service.

Knowledge

3. Demonstrate some of the musical exercises that you use to practice your skills.

4. Talk about your instrument and why you enjoy playing it (or the songs you sing and why you enjoy singing them).

5. Talk about some of the musicians who are associated with your instrument.

Interest

6. Talk about your own interests in music, including what you listen to most, and how this is similar to or different from the music you play or sing.

MUSICIAN – STAGE 5

Complete the following:

Skill

1. Achieve Grade Five of the Associated Board of the Royal School of Music (or similar) on the instrument of your choice.

Performance

2. Sing or play three different types of song or tune on your chosen instrument. One should be a solo and one of the other two should accompany other musicians in an arrangement of their choice. The performance should be public, such as at a Group Show, school concert or church service.

Knowledge

3. Demonstrate some of the musical exercises that you use to practice your skills.

4. Talk about your instrument and why you enjoy playing it (or the songs you sing and why you enjoy singing them).

5. Name several well-known pieces of music associated with your instrument.

6. Name several musicians who are associated with your instrument.

Interest

7. Talk about your own interests in music, including what you listen to most and how this is similar to or different from the music you play or sing.

→ NIGHTS AWAY

Complete the requirements below:

Nights Away 1

Complete one night away as part of a recognised Scout activity, sleeping either in tents, bivouacs, hostels, on boats or other centres.

Nights Away 5

Complete five nights away on recognised Scout activities, sleeping in either tents, bivouacs, hostels, on boats or other centres.

Nights Away 10

Complete 10 nights away on recognised Scout activities, sleeping either in tents, bivouacs, hostels, on boats or other centres.

Nights Away 20

Complete 20 nights away on recognised Scout activities, sleeping either in tents, bivouacs, hostels, on boats or other centres.

Nights Away 35

Complete 35 nights away on recognised Scout activities, sleeping either in tents, bivouacs, hostels, on boats or other centres.

Nights Away 50

Complete 50 nights away on recognised Scout activities, sleeping either in tents, bivouacs, hostels, on boats or other centres.

Nights Away 75

Complete 75 nights away on recognised Scout activities, sleeping either in tents, bivouacs, hostels, on boats or other centres.

Nights Away 100

Complete 100 nights away on recognised Scout activities, sleeping either in tents, bivouacs, hostels, on boats or other centres.

Nights Away 125

Complete 125 nights away on recognised Scout activities, sleeping either in tents, bivouacs, hostels, on boats or other centres.

Nights Away 150

Complete 150 nights away on recognised Scout activities, sleeping either in tents, bivouacs, hostels, on boats or other centres.

Nights Away 175

Complete 175 nights away on recognised Scout activities, sleeping either in tents, bivouacs, hostels, on boats or other centres.

Nights Away 200

Complete 200 nights away on recognised Scout activities, sleeping either in tents, bivouacs, hostels, on boats or other centres.

Notes: Young people of any Section may, with the agreement of their Leader, also include nights away spent on educational trips, Duke of Edinburgh Award Expeditions and other similar excursions.

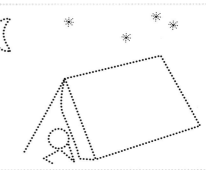

→ # SWIMMER – STAGES 1-5

Complete the requirements below:

SWIMMER – STAGE 1

Complete the following:

Safety

1. Know the safety rules and where it is safe to swim locally.

Enter pool

2. Without using the steps, demonstrate a controlled entry into at least 1.5 metres of water.

Short swim

3. Swim ten metres on your front.

Tread water

4. Tread water for 30 seconds in a vertical position.

Water skills

5. Using a buoyancy aid, float still in the water for 30 seconds.

6. Demonstrate your ability to retrieve an object from chest deep water.

7. Perform a push and glide on both your front and back.

Distance swim

8. Swim 25 metres without stopping.

Swimming activity

9. Take part in an organised swimming activity.

SWIMMER – STAGE 2

Complete the following:

Safety

1. Know the safety rules and where it is safe to swim locally.

Enter pool

2. Demonstrate a controlled entry or dive from the side of the pool, into at least 1.5 metres of water.

Short swim

3. Swim ten metres on your front, ten metres on your back, and ten metres on your back using only your legs.

Tread water

4. Tread water for three minutes in a vertical position.

Water skills

5. Surface dive into at least 1.5 metres of water and touch the bottom with both hands.

6. Mushroom float for ten seconds.

7. Enter the pool and push off from the side on your front and glide for five metres.

8. From the side of the pool, push off on your back and glide for as far as possible.

Distance swim

9. Swim 100 metres without stopping.

Swimming activity

10. Take part in an organised swimming activity.

SWIMMER – STAGE 3

Complete the following:

Safety

1. Know the safety rules and where it is safe to swim locally.

2. Explain the rules governing swimming for Scouts.

Enter pool

3. Demonstrate a controlled entry or dive from the side of the pool into at least 1.5 metres of water.

Short swim

4. Swim 50 metres in shirt and shorts.

Tread water

5. Tread water for three minutes with one hand behind your back.

Water skills

6. Surface dive into 1.5 metres of water and recover an object with both hands from the bottom. Return to the side of the pool holding the object in both hands.

7. Enter the water from the side of the pool by sliding in from a sitting position. Using any floating object for support, take up and hold the Heat Escape Lessening Posture for five minutes.

Distance swim

8. Swim 400 metres without stopping.

Swimming activity

9. Take part in an organised swimming activity, since gaining your previous Swimmer Badge.

SWIMMER - STAGE 4

Complete the following:

Safety

1. Know the safety rules and where it is safe to swim locally.

2. Explain the rules covering swimming for Scouts.

Enter pool

3. Demonstrate a racing dive into at least 1.5 metres of water and straddle jump into at least two meters of water.

Short swim

4. Swim 100 metres in less than four minutes.

Tread water

5. Tread water for five minutes.

Water skills

6. Surface dive into 1.5 metres of water, both head first and feet first and swim at least five metres under water on both occasions.

7. Enter the water as for unknown depth. Swim ten metres to a floating object and use it to take up and hold the Heat Escape Lessening Posture for five minutes.

Distance Swim

8. Swim 800 metres without stopping. You should swim 400 metres on your front and 400 metres on your back.

Swimming activity

9. Take part in an organised swimming activity, since gaining your previous Swimmer Badge.

SWIMMER - STAGE 5

Complete the following:

Safety

1. Know the safety rules and where it is safe to swim locally.

2. Explain the rules governing swimming for Scouts.

Enter pool

3. Demonstrate a racing dive into at least 1.5 metres of water and straddle jump into at least two meters of water.

Short swim

4. Swim 100 metres in shirt and shorts. On completion, remove the additional clothes and climb out of the pool unaided. Time limit: three minutes.

Tread water

5. Tread water for five minutes, for three of which one arm must be held clear of the water.

Water skills

6. Scull on your back, head first for ten metres then feet first for ten metres. Move into a tuck position and keeping your head out of the water, turn 360 degrees.

7. Swim ten metres, perform a somersault without touching the side of the pool and continue to swim in the same direction for a further ten metres.

8. Demonstrate the Heat Escape Lessening Posture.

9. Demonstrate a surface dive, both head and feet first into 1.5 metres of water.

Distance Swim

10. Swim 1000 metres using any three recognised strokes for a minimum distance of 200 metres per stroke. This swim must be completed in 35 minutes.

Swimming activity

11. Take part in an organised swimming activity, since gaining your previous Swimmer Badge.

→ ACTIVITY PLUS BADGES

Silver edge

Activity PLUS badges can be awarded if you develop your skills or knowledge to a higher level than the Activity Badge. It should represent a significant achievement, taking into account your abilities and the nature of the activity, as well as local facilities.

Complete the requirements below:

1. Hold the relevant Activity Badge.

2. Agree a target with the Troop leadership team before seeking to gain a PLUS badge, This should involve taking part in additional training or involvement in the activity, in order to develop further your knowledge and/or skills.

Examples of appropriate targets might be:

- For the Canoeist PLUS, achieve the Paddlepower Discover

- For the Pulling PLUS take charge of a boat under oars

- For the Meteorologist PLUS, keep a weather diary for an agreed number of months

- For the Dragon Boating PLUS, train for a month as part of a team to compete in a National Dragon Boat Competition

3. Achieve the target to the satisfaction of the Troop leadership team.

Note: *Policy, Organisation and Rules* and relevant Activity factsheets should be referred to where appropriate.

A PLUS badge can be awarded for any Activity Badge, apart from the following:

- Any Staged Activity Badge

- Basic Aviation skills

- Aviation Skills

- Advanced Aviation Skills

- Basic Nautical Skills

- Nautical Skills

- Advanced Nautical Skills

→ INSTRUCTOR BADGES

Gold edge

Instructor Badges are available for Scouts, and can be achieved for almost all Activity Badges.

The requirements are as follows:

1. Hold the Activity Badge.

2. Have enough knowledge of the Activity Badge requirements to allow you to instruct a Scout in that subject.

3. Attend a training course covering the technical skills involved in the Activity Badge and the use of appropriate training methods.

4. Assist with the training of Scouts in the subject over a period of at least three months.

Notes:

Requirements 1, 2 and 3 must be completed before you can begin requirement 4.

For those subjects that do not have a recognised technical skill course, an individual training programme can be arranged with a suitably qualified instructor.

If you have already gained an Instructor Badge, you may be exempt from the training methods section of the third requirement.

It may not be possible to gain an Instructor Badge in some areas, such as Parascending, where there are clear age restrictions.

→ PARTNERSHIP AWARDS

ENVIRONMENT PARTNERSHIP AWARD

The Environment Partnership Award is about developing a way of life that does not harm the environment, in other words, a sustainable lifestyle. It is designed to bring a group together to promote an environmentally friendly way of living. The award aims to:

- Promote environmental awareness in young people
- Support the environmental focus in the Balanced Programme
- Ensure there is a positive influence on everyone taking part
- Have a long-term benefit on sustainable development globally or locally.

INTERNATIONAL PARTNERSHIP AWARD

The International Partnership Award is about developing friendships, but not just international ones! The aim is to encourage friendship and links, both within the Section and internationally. By working together on this Award, everyone will grow in understanding and respect for each other. You will also make new friends and find out about people living in other countries.

The International Partnership Award opens up new horizons in the Balanced Programme for all Sections. It can be worked towards at the same time as the Global Challenge. The aims of the Award are to:

- Promote international activities for all Sections
- Support the international focus in the Programme
- Ensure there is a positive influence on everyone taking part
- Have a long term benefit for people living in another country.

FAITH PARTNERSHIP AWARD

The Faith Partnership Award is about encouraging young people to develop an understanding of their own or another faith community. It is designed to bring a group together to promote a greater understanding of the life, history or practices of a faith community in your local community.

The aims of the Faith Partnership Award are to:

- Develop a greater understanding of a faith community
- Support activities in the Beliefs and Attitudes Programme Zone
- Make sure there is a positive faith influence on everyone taking part
- Have a long-term benefit in encouraging greater understanding and awareness of a local faith community.

Requirements of the three awards:

1. Identify a partner and a project or activity that relates to the themed area – Environment, Faith or International Partnership.
2. Together with those involved, set objectives for what you wish to achieve and plan the project.
3. Take part in and successfully complete the joint activity.
4. Assess the benefits to those involved.
5. Award the Partnership Award to those young people taking part.

Partners
A partner may be from within Scouting or an appropriate external organisation.

→ GLOSSARY

→ TROOP TERMS

Activity Permit Scheme

This scheme ensures that those who wish to lead or supervise adventurous activities have the ability and experience to do so.

Appointment Advisory Committee

A mandatory sub-committee of a District or County/Area Executive Committee responsible for providing advice on a number of aspects related to adult appointments.

Appointment Holder

An adult volunteer who has successfully been through The Scout Association's adult appointment process and has been appointed to carry out a particular role in Scouting.

Assistant Patrol Leader

A Scout who assists a Patrol Leader with the leadership of a Patrol in the Scout Troop.

Associate Member

An adult who wishes to join Scouting, but not take the Promise. Associate Members cannot hold Leader or Commissioner appointments, as these appointments require the individual to be a Member.

Beaver Scout

An invested Member of the Movement in the Beaver Scout Section.

Beaver Scout Leader

This is the appointment held by a Leader responsible for the running of a Beaver Scout Colony. Adults may adopt other names to use with children e.g. Brown Beaver, Big Beaver, Grey Beaver.

Beaver Scout Section

The first Section in the Scout Group, with a core age range of 6-8. Children can join at 5¾ and remain until 8½ years.

Cub Scout

An Invested Member of the Movement in the Cub Scout Section.

Cub Scout Section

The second Section in the Scout Group, with a core age of 8-10½ years.

Explorer Belt

This is a programme element of the Explorer Scout and Scout Network programme, which encourages explanation in another country. If the activity is successful, the Explorer Belt is awarded.

Explorer Scout

An invested Member of the Movement in the Explorer Scout Section, usually aged between 14 and 18 years of age.

Badges and Awards
Participation Awards
Chief Scout's Gold Award
Challenge Badges
Activity Badges
Staged Activity Badges
Activity Plus Badges
Instructor Badges
Partnership Awards
Glossary

Explorer Scout Section

The fourth Scout Section, the Explorer Scout Section is delivered by Scout Districts, although Units can be linked with Scout Groups. The core age range is 14-18 years, with young people able to join at 13½ and remain until 18½ years.

Fall in

An instruction used primarily in the Scout Troop to bring young people together.

Group Chairman

The title of a person nominated annually by the Group Scout Leader who chairs the Scout Group Executive Committee and Group Council.

Induction

A support programme for adults new to Scouting or those taking up a new role.

Joining In Award

A badge awarded to a Beaver Scout or Cub Scout for participating in a Balanced Programme, normally over a period of 12 months.

Line manager

The person to whom an adult is responsible. For example, the line manager of a Beaver Scout Leader is the Group Scout Leader. The line manager provides adults with guidance, support and encouragement.

National Governing Body

An outside organisation recognised by the Sports Council as governing organisation of an activity. National Governing Bodies often provide qualifications recognised by The Scout Association.

Participation Award

These are badges awarded annually to members of the Scout or Explorer Scout Sections for participating in a Balanced Programme.

Patrol

The name given to a group of Scouts within a Scout Troop.

Patrol Leader

A Scout who leads a Patrol in the Scout Troop.

Patrol Forum

A meeting of members of a Patrol, in the Scout Troop.

Patron

Her Majesty, Queen Elizabeth II is the Patron of The Scout Association of the United Kingdom.

Programme Review

A method by which adults in Scouting can review and plan their programmes. This will ensure that a Balanced Programme is being offered to young people.

President

The Duke of Kent has been President of The Scout Association of the United Kingdom since 1975.

Scout

An invested Member of the Movement normally aged 10½ to 14 years of age. This is also a generic term used to describe any Member of the Scout Movement.

Scout Leader

The adult Leader responsible for the running of a Scout Troop.

Scout Network Member

An invested member of the Movement, normally aged 18-25 years of age.

Scout Network Section

The fifth and final youth section, the Network Section is delivered by Counties or Districts. The core age range is 18-25 years.

Scout Section

The original Section, as founded by Baden-Powell, and the final Section within the Scout Group. With a core age range of 10½ to 14½, young people can join at 10 years and remain until their 15th birthday.

Scout Salute

Members use the Scout Salute to salute a flag when it is broken and at other ceremonies.

Section Assistant

An adult who supports the Leader or Assistant Leader with the running of a particular Section.

Silver Acorn

An award given to adults for especially distinguished service. It also has a Bar, which may be awarded after not less than five years of further distinguished service.

Sixer

A Cub Scout who leads a Six in a Cub Pack.

Skills Instructor

People appointed to instruct young people on specific skills such as climbing, canoeing or First Aid.

Troop

The collective name for Scouts (10½ to 14 year olds) meeting together as a Section.

Young Leader

An Explorer Scout working in the Beaver, Cub or Scout Sections as part of that Section's leadership team. A Young Leader is required to undertake Young Leader training and may be part of a Young Leader Unit.

PROGRAMME METHODS

[SCOUTS]

PROGRAMME ZONES

Programme Methods: Activities Outdoors · Games · Design & creativity · Visits & visitors · Service · Technology & new skills · Team building activities · Activities with others · Themes · Prayer worship & reflection

Programme Zones: Outdoor & Adventure · Global · Community · Fit for Life · Creative Expression · Beliefs & Attitudes

The Bottom Line: Activity · Fun · Teamwork · Leadership · Relationships · Commitment · Personal development

1 tick = Poor
2 ticks = Good
3 ticks = Excellent